ROBERT A. ROHM, Ph.D.
and STEWART W. CROSS

SPONSOR WITH *Style*

Secret Steps to Personality Insights
for Sponsoring and Coaching

PERSONALITY
INSIGHTS

Project editor - Julie Anne Cross

Cover designer - Carol Dunlop

Layout and Graphics - Julie & Stewart Cross

Credits:

photos: cover by Photo Disk and Body Shop
photos: page 23, by Rick Diamond
Be a People Person by John C. Maxwell
Telemarketers Training Manual by TeleCross Corporation
An Enterprising Life by Jay Van Andel
Success for Dummies by Zig Ziglar

Published by Personality Insights, Inc.

PO Box 28592 • Atlanta, GA 30358-0592
(800) 509-*DISC* • http://www.personality-insights.com

ISBN 0-9641080-4-6

First Edition: March 1999
Second Edition: June 1999

Printed in the United States of America

This book is lovingly dedicated to our children:

Rachael, Esther, Elizabeth, Susanna
Rohm

and

Wesley, Ethan, Rosanne, Jason
Cross

Contents

Foreword

Technology changes the way business is done. In the Industrial Revolution, machines were developed that changed the way people worked. Suddenly, the sunlight made no difference as to when people could work. In an agricultural society, farmers had worked from sun up to sun down. Technology changed peoples' lives because machines could run at night just as well as in the daytime. Those with the vision to see what this machinery might do for them were able to take advantage of this change. They led the way, showing people how to make the transition into this new way of life. This is how these leaders prospered and became wealthy. Many others who could not or would not make this change suffered greatly for it. Some went out of business. Some lost their livelihood. Some simply never knew what they had missed. Machines were here to stay, and people learned how to live with the changes that had come with them.

In the Information Age, electronic communication has been developed that is once again changing the way people work. Now location makes little difference as to where people work. In an industrial society, people had to go to a factory or office to work. The Internet is changing peoples' lives because now people can function electronically no matter where they are. You can fax a letter to someone and they will receive it almost immediately. E-mail has opened the way for orders to be placed and goods to be shipped in the same day. Those with the vision to see what this method of communication might do for them will be able to take advantage of this change. They will be the ones to prosper. This is what we want to be able to do with you! We want you to lead the way with us, showing people how to make the transition into this new way of life. As we lead, we will prosper together. Electronic communication is growing every day, and we are learning how to live with the changes that come with it. This is a great opportunity for all of us!

We see one thing that will never change. Technology will not replace people! As technology advances, we must work even harder to maintain strong relationships with the people who are important to us. As my wife Kathy says, "The most important thing in building a successful organization is understanding people. And the people at Personality Insights can help you do this better than anyone I know!" I totally agree. This is the reason why this book is so vital to your success, and why I plan to promote it everywhere I go!

God bless you,

Jody Victor

Publisher's Preface

I began to share my understanding of personality styles with several leaders in the Amway business in the same way that I had learned about them. I was excited to show them how understanding personality styles had helped my relationship with my daughter Rachael. I knew that this understanding would help them in their businesses too. As one leader saw the power in understanding personality styles through the style assessments of his business staff, he told me, "Since we started using these personality profiles, our work productivity has increased. I'm not spending my time subjectively trying to figure out what's going on at our office. Now I have a tool to evaluate our staff objectively and know exactly what I can do to motivate them."

I was grateful that I could help him, and encouraged by his results. Then he asked, "If we gave you all of our business, could you handle it?" I said, "Sure!" I didn't have a clue then what "all of our business" meant, but I was anxious to get started! As our association grew from one Diamond organization to another, I grew by seeing the vastness of this great Amway enterprise. I was impressed with the simple genius of the Amway Compensation Plan and the power of sharing it with others. The incredible number and variety of quality products and services that are available through the business surprised me. But I knew that the Plan and the products were just part of the foundation for building a business. Independent Business Owners also needed effective people skills as they pursued their dreams.

This *Sponsor with Style* book began after many leaders asked us for specific information on Independent Business Owners' (IBOs') personality style issues. Judging from the positive feedback we received from numerous Diamonds, I know this book will make a helpful contribution to your success. In offering these insights, our purpose is not to instruct you on how to show the Plan or build your business, because your upline has established the proven pattern you should follow. Rather, we want to make our contribution in your relationships, showing you the personality insights you need to realize your dreams and goals.

Personality styles impact many areas of your business: your ability to establish rapport upline and build your downline, to set goals and to organize your work. Your personality style even reveals the ways you respond to the obstacles you must face and overcome as you grow and achieve your dreams.

I would like to extend my sincere appreciation to the Diamonds who have understood the potential of these personality insights in the business. They have trusted us to share this information with their groups at conferences, in training tapes and through recommended books. It is a sacred trust to be allowed to teach another person how to live a rewarding life. I have experienced first hand how much the Diamonds love their people and want the very best for them. I have been privileged to walk with these giants. We have really enjoyed talking with many Independent Business Owners about their business and personal relationships. It has been our privilege to help them understand themselves and others and to learn with them how to use these personality insights effectively.

I especially want to thank the Personality Insights staff for their vital contribution to our team as we put together this book, *Sponsor with Style*. As I speak at functions, they entertain questions and discuss ideas with many Independent Business Owners. Rick Herceg, our director of customer service, is responsible for our Personality Insights function information and book table. Rick has been my dear friend and brother in all I have done in life. We have worked together in some capacity for over thirty years. (He is getting old!) We have traveled all over the world together. He is a tireless worker who walks his talk. There are not many like him left on this planet. Everyone should be so blessed as I have been to have such a special, caring, committed friend like Rick.

The firsthand knowledge and experience of our staff has also become part of this book. Stewart Cross brings business and sales expertise and experience to this book and to our business as our general manager. Stewart has a great business mind and is such a good role model. As a high *D* type, he *pushes* me every day to be a better person. I have learned much from the example of *balance* in his own personal life. His good ideas are practical, helpful and profitable. Julie Anne Cross, as our editor, makes sure that our products, and especially this book, are clear, concise and communicate our exciting information. Mere words cannot express my gratitude and appreciation to Julie. She adds so much to our team. She has been a part of Personality Insights, Inc., for several years. She works here *full time*, is a *full time* wife and a *full time* mother. How many *full time*s can there be?! She has a pleasant spirit and she is smart. Stewart and Julie's four teenage children are emotionally healthy, academically alert and spiritually sound. Stewart married way over his head! I love them both very much. I am grateful God sent them to help this organization.

Carl Smith, in our marketing and sales, enjoys interacting with the special people who are part of this business. As the newest member of our team, he brings a warm personal touch to helping all of our customers. Our support staff, including Nancy Enis, my administrative assistant, and Kea Eason, our marketing assistant, are special to me and are vital to our team.

Most of all, my thanks to you, the reader, for the opportunity to serve you through this book. I am eager to see you succeed in building a successful business. Your family and friends will share this exciting journey with you as you learn to understand yourself and others together. Your story of personal growth and achievement can then be shared with other Independent Business Owners. I know you will get that chance to share as you move on in the business. One day, I hope we will share a stage together, encouraging others to become everything God meant for them to be. Who knows... maybe when you "go Diamond," you will invite me to speak at one of your functions! God bless you!

Robert A. Rohm

Robert A. Rohm, Ph.D.
President - Publisher

Introduction

Imagine for a moment that your long lost aunt died. In her will she has left you ten million dollars, on the condition that you spend it within one year. You must also spend it on things that you think will make you happy for the rest of your life. What would you buy?

Perhaps you would buy a fabulous home, that sports car you always wanted, a dream vacation to see that exotic place you would love to see. Maybe you would buy your way into the Oscars, just to rub shoulders with the stars... How would you spend *any* amount of money so that you would be *truly* happy? We do not know about you, but we would love to try!

Some people win the lottery, and they do get to try. Surprisingly, most of those people spend all that money within a couple of years and are no better off than when they started. Why? Because the most valuable things in our lives are *intangible* — we cannot buy them, or even touch them, but they do come at a price.

The most valuable things in our lives are the people we become, the relationships we enjoy, and the lasting contributions we give to our world. We all search for security and significance, the security of knowing that *who I am really matters* and that *my world is a better place because I am here.*

As you grow in this business, something exciting happens. You grow into a winner, a leader, and a coach. Your world expands to include dream possessions, exciting experiences, and positive people. You have the unique opportunity to become significant in the lives of others as you enjoy an ever-expanding world.

How do you become that Diamond-valued person, enjoying lasting relationships and making significant contributions to our world? It starts with you. It starts with your relationship with your spouse, or family, or friends. It starts in your business. Are we back in your real world now?

Many of the recurring frustrations in building your business can be linked to people. Your IBOs may not see eye-to-eye with you on important issues that can affect their success — and yours! They won't respond as you wish they would. They will have ongoing challenges which you think you could easily resolve. Has this thought ever occurred to you: "What is the matter with the people I am in business with? Why can't they be normal... like me?"

How Does this Happen?

At a recent function, one very successful Emerald confessed, "You know, I've probably chased off as many people as I've brought in." He was saying his *style* was as repellent to some as it was magnetic to others. When we don't seem to fit in with prospects or IBOs, we can tend to "write them off" as quitters or losers. When someone quits or doesn't get in, it is not always because of something we did. But many leaders have said that there was a time when they might have chosen to fail rather than succeed. The thin threads holding them in this business were woven by a leader who helped them hear the right things, give the right responses, and find the right help. They had a leader who had built a strong relationship with them, and knew how to keep them on their team.

A wise coach knows the players. But the actions and attitudes of some IBOs seem beyond knowing! When we do not understand how and why people think the way they do, we have difficulty trusting them. We can become frustrated when people do not meet our expectations or fail to grow under our leadership. How does this happen? What can we do about it?

We want to start with you in your real world. We'll help you grow to improve your relationships and build real teams, groups who work together to create something better than any one of them alone could create.

Sponsor with Style! will introduce you to your **Personality Quotient** and empower you with:

🄿🅀 Four Steps to Raising your PQ

1. Understanding yourself through your personality style

2. Understanding another person through their personality style

3. Adapting your style to have better relationships

4. Building better teams where *Together Everyone Achieves More!*

As you read, you will see the actions and reactions of others from a new perspective. You will begin to understand them as you have never before been able to do. You may begin to think about how they see you too. Take the action plans and work through them, and have fun exploring what you can do to take these concepts into your real world. We know how helpful they have been in our lives. We are excited that maybe, one day, we will meet you at a function and have the privilege of learning how they have helped you to grow too!

Here are a few suggestions for how to get the most from this book

- *As you are reading, we want to encourage you to highlight and make notes in your book. Interacting with the ideas presented will bring these insights into your world, where you can grow by using them.*

- *Understanding personalities as we do, we know that some people are "skimmers" rather than readers. We have placed icons in the margins next to the information you should be sure to read. Even if you read every word, these icons will help you find memorable reference points for you.*

HERE IS WHAT EACH OF THE FOUR ICONS MEANS:

 This Take Action icon marks something that you can pick up and run with now!

 This Powerful Idea icon identifies an important concept which will be key to your understanding.

 The Thinker icon says "Take some time to think about this!" You may want to discuss what you are thinking and doing in this regard with your upline leaders.

 This Closer Look icon points out further information that you may wish to explore. Further resources are available to you through Personality Insights, Inc., or your upline organization.

Experience has taught us that you cannot grasp every concept in a new book all at once. Therefore, please make a commitment to use *each week* one new concept that you explore in the Personal Action Planners located at the end of each chapter. By the end of the year, you will have over 50 new success strategies that help you build your organization. Let's get started!

Understanding Human Behavior

The Information Age allows us to communicate at an ever-increasing rate. This is an exciting time in which to live! E-mail and faxes can be sent instantaneously. Cellular phones and pagers keep many people just a phone call away. With all this great technology, we might expect to have fewer problems with understanding one another, but in fact, the reverse seems to be true. This may be true because we spend little time just *spending time together*, and also perhaps because we interact with an ever increasing number of people.

We still care very much about people and want to understand how to get along together. How can we do this? Understanding human behavior and the predictable patterns that we can observe in our personalities can really help us better understand ourselves and others. We can have a better picture of our own natural perspective on life and begin to see how different the perspectives of others can be.

Over twenty-four hundred years ago, keen observers of people began to notice that there are predictable patterns of behavior. In time, this observation led to the Model of Human Behavior that we use to understand these patterns. The following charts review this model, and are a ready reference for you as you read this book.

Each of us has a motor that drives us. It has a fast pace that makes us more Outgoing, or it has a slow pace that makes us more Reserved. In the illustration on the right, the arrows indicate that lighter shading, closer to the midline, shows less intensity in this motor activity. You may be extremely Outgoing or Reserved, or you may be just moderately Outgoing or Reserved.

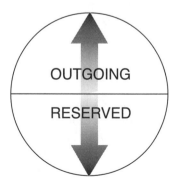

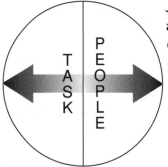

Just as we have a motor that drives us, we also have a compass that draws us toward either Task or People. Because we are drawn toward either task or people, we are either task-oriented or people-oriented. In the illustration on the left, the arrows indicate that lighter shading, closer to the midline, shows less intensity in this compass activity. You may be extremely people-oriented or task-oriented, or you may be just moderately people-oriented or task-oriented.

When we put together both the Motor and Compass Activity models, we see the Model of Human Behavior illustrated at right. We see that:

the **D** type is outgoing and task-oriented
the **I** type is outgoing and people-oriented
the **S** type is reserved and people-oriented
the **C** type is reserved and task-oriented

Each **DISC** type has a group of descriptive words called *traits* that are used to describe that *type*. You will recognize the most important of these traits as the **D**ominant, **I**nspiring, **S**upportive, and **C**autious descriptive word groups in the following chart. These *traits* describe a **DISC** *type*, but each person who has that type has some of these traits in their personality style. *Style* describes your personality style. Your personality style may have more than one type in it. Your special blend of more than one high type is called your *Style Blend*. Just one more term before we go on! We also use the word *Combination* to describe what happens when two different people interact with each other.

PERSONALITY STYLE BLENDS

Only a very small percentage of people have a personality style that is predominantly just one **DISC** type. While only one **DISC** type may be highest in your style, about 80% of people also have a secondary **DISC** type that helps and influences the predominant type in their style. If one has a highest **I** type and a secondary **S** type, we would say that

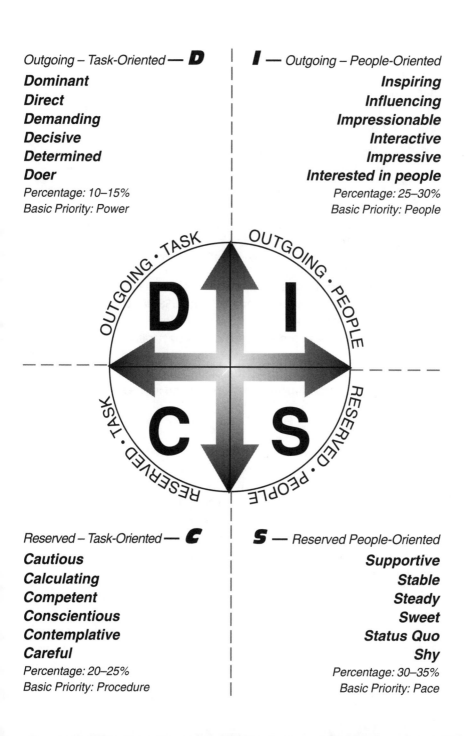

Outgoing – Task-Oriented — **D**

Dominant
Direct
Demanding
Decisive
Determined
Doer
Percentage: 10–15%
Basic Priority: Power

I *— Outgoing – People-Oriented*

Inspiring
Influencing
Impressionable
Interactive
Impressive
Interested in people
Percentage: 25–30%
Basic Priority: People

Reserved – Task-Oriented — **C**

Cautious
Calculating
Competent
Conscientious
Contemplative
Careful
Percentage: 20–25%
Basic Priority: Procedure

S *— Reserved People-Oriented*

Supportive
Stable
Steady
Sweet
Status Quo
Shy
Percentage: 30–35%
Basic Priority: Pace

they have an *I/S* Style Blend. It is less common, but not highly un-usual, to have a third high type in your Style Blend. You may have felt that you could easily identify with traits from more than one **DISC** type when you read the descriptive traits of each of the types, and your Style Blend will show this.

 If you have completed a personality profile, please turn to the Appendix at the end of the book to record your graphs and find a more complete description of your graphs. If you have not completed a personality profile, you may want to use the form at the end of the book to order yours now.

The book *Who Do You Think You Are... Anyway*? also supplies a great deal of information about understanding your style blend. We recommend that you complete a custom-prepared SUCCESSment™ Profile Report, identifying with great accuracy how your blend operates in life and business. It will reveal the strengths you naturally possess and the struggles you may face in adapting your style, with specific suggestions for creating an action plan that you can use for greater business success. Ordering information is found in the back of this book.

PERSONALITY COMBINATIONS

When we interact, your style blend and my style blend come together in combination. Whether for work or for fun, if we can understand each other better we can enjoy one another more and be more productive, too. Our book, *Who Do You Think You Are... Anyway*?, explains many of the factors that work for and against harmony in our rela-tionships, based on how our blends get along. In this book we will specifically explore how combinations of different styles affect showing the Plan, receiving coaching, and coaching downline.

What great news, that we can all learn to adapt our styles! We can have greater success with anyone we meet, whatever their style. These personality insights can help you be more effective in the business, and any time you are involved with people, which is most of the time! Use these personality insights to gain a larger perspective on how you present and represent your business as you receive coaching upline for your growing business.

PICTURE THIS!

"This is a powerful book! Start now and you'll get great results!"

"Ha! People will love this book! I'm so excited about the fun we'll have!"

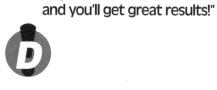

"Smile... We'll just pace ourselves through this book. This will be easy together."

"Hmmm...Let's think about the correct procedures we can learn from this book..."

This is a great time to be in this business! You and your organization can expect great things as you practice these personality insights!

Getting Down To Business...

Achieving Success with People

The Start...

"I am learning to understand myself better through learning about my personality style."

"I am learning to recognize the perspectives of other personality styles by observing others."

"I am learning to appreciate and accept the differences in the personality styles of my family."

"I am starting to adjust my style so I can better meet the needs of those close to me."

"I am beginning to put this information to work for me as I seek my upline's coaching for presenting the Plan."

"I am considering ways to encourage my downline according to their needs."

"I am focusing on the great results I have when I consistently work in the business."

"I am becoming more aware of effective ways to relate to the people who are important in my business."

The Goal...!

CHAPTER ONE

The Three Ps

You became a part of the Amway opportunity because someone had a dream. It was their dream, a dream for a better way of living. Part of their dream was sharing it with you. They believed they had great **Products**, believed they had a **Plan** that would benefit you, and believed you were one of the **People** with whom they wanted to work. You saw their dream and, in time, you began to dream too! You needed the **Products**, the **Plan**, and the **People** to make this dream come true.

Most people find it very easy to understand the products and the Plan. If we asked you what *Zoom* would clean, you could find an easy answer. After seeing the Plan presented once or twice, you could also tell us the basic concepts of the Plan. It is more difficult to understand why the Plan or products may appeal to someone else. How do you know what will benefit them? The dynamics of personality styles will help you know where to start. For example, you may really appreciate how *Zoom* cleans your golf club heads, but if someone else doesn't care about keeping golf clubs clean, this will mean nothing to them. You may also dream of building a business so that you can have that red convertible, but if your friends hate to have windblown hair, they may dream of a luxury sedan instead. How do you find what will really attract someone to the business? This is what personality insights are all about.

Through the years of speaking at weekend functions, we have shared the three Ps in this business: the products, the Plan, and the people. We can easily see how personality insights relate to the people, but as we look more closely you will see that personality insights greatly influence the products, as well as the Plan. Developing personality insights into the customers, the prospects, and even yourself will greatly influence and affect every step in the process of selling products, showing the Plan, and making your business grow— by helping your people grow.

THE PRODUCTS

The first **P** is the Products. Every businessperson must fully understand their product line. In a sales study, top producers from various fields revealed one thing in common: they believed in what they were selling. They were sold on their own product. Their daily goal was not to convince someone else that they needed their product, but simply to share their own belief. This, in turn sold the products! A friend of Dr. Rohm's who was the top Toyota salesman in Dallas, Texas, illustrates this when he says, "I never try to sell Toyotas... because *I am already sold* on them! I simply go for rides with potential customers, telling them all about my Toyota and how much I love it! Then we come back to the car lot and they buy one! It is really very simple!" He knows and believes in his product, doesn't he?

Remember that *people* sell products; products do not sell themselves. People must understand product features and communicate the benefits those products will provide to the customer. We will discuss features and benefits in Chapter 12, but now we will focus on each personality type and product knowledge.

How can two people look at the same product and see something different? Each personality type sees product knowledge from a different perspective, because each type looks for different benefits from those products. The **D** type person will have the natural tendency to look at the business opportunity and think that he or she will understand the products well enough to sell them to someone else. After all, with such a great business opportunity, why wouldn't anyone start buying from themselves everything they could buy?! Other styles may want to know how well the products work and how to best use them, before ordering them. Taking the time to study the product line, by listing the features and how they benefit the customer, would strengthen the **D**s ability to intelligently answer questions and objections that are sure to arise. The **D** type will want to jump past these questions, but experience shows that good products must be available, or in time the customer will begin to shop elsewhere. The *I* type person will naturally talk about the wonderful products. They may give the impression that they know about all of them. Such a large, successful corporation wouldn't sell a product that doesn't work, now would it? In reality, the products that the *I* types have actually used themselves are the ones they will be most excited about! Watching product demonstrations at functions will help the *I* type gain a working knowledge of the products and increase their credibility. The *S* type person will want a thorough understanding of the products simply to support their customer with guaranteed customer benefits. The *S* type will gain confidence by remembering how much they appreciate using these great products. Their friends will appreciate using these products too. They may need to be reminded to stop studying and get out and actually talk to prospects! The *C* type will carefully conduct an in-depth study listing so many features that the customer benefits get lost. They will need to remember not to overwhelm their customer with too much detail. Only another *C* type will be interested in all that data! When the *C* type chooses the three or four best benefits that they have experienced to share with someone else, they will leave the door open for that friend to ask for more information at a later time.

We all need product knowledge, but balance in our approach to gaining and using product knowledge is essential to success. Imagine what happens when an *I* tries to impress a *C* with these *great* products. The *C* quickly knows that the *I* is really excited, but doesn't know what he's talking about. On the other hand, the *S* may get up the courage to talk to a *D* prospect about products. The *S* may be scared off when the *D* wants to just try some *Zoom* and then get back later to the *S*. Can you see how product knowledge is also affected by personality styles?

We most commonly think about product knowledge in reference to retail sales to customers, but interactive distribution concepts encourage us to remember that *we* are our own *best customer*. Product knowledge really starts with us! Think about the last time you went into a grocery store. Even with limited product knowledge of many items we purchase from local stores, we always try to find and purchase products that benefit us. As Independent Business Owners, we can access a broad base of product knowledge to make informed purchases. Armed with this knowledge, it is easier to change where we shop and begin to buy from ourselves. Our firsthand experience with products will encourage a second source for sales – our own IBOs. When we tell them about that new product we just love, they will try it too! As they buy from themselves they are gaining product knowledge that they can share with others too.

THE PLAN

The second *P* is the Plan. To most IBOs, "Show the Plan" means presenting the Compensation Plan in the same way that it was shown to them by their Sponsor. Even though the Plan is presented with the same facts and figures, each personality type will approach showing the Plan differently. Understanding your own personality style will help you to understand your own strengths and struggles as they relate to successfully showing the Plan.

Different types will approach showing the Plan in some very different ways. To the *S* type, showing the Plan may be intimidating — they may wonder, "Will I remember where all the bonus numbers fit in, and can I explain how PV/BV works?" They need to bear in mind that everyone will make a few mistakes the first few times. In showing the Plan, just like in any type of presentation, repetition and practice is perhaps the best teacher. Knowing that their sponsor was such a good friend to share this opportunity with them, and that their prospect will see how much they care, will help them relax when they share this opportunity, too.

The *D*, on the other hand, won't be intimidated! The *D* will think, "Hey, I saw the Plan presented to me and I signed up immediately! I understand how powerful it is; in fact, I will add to it and I'll make it even better!" The *D* will aggressively present the Plan! Getting out and talking to people will be their strength. Their sponsor will want to help them gain confidence in the system as it is, before considering too many creative changes. The *D* may need encouragement to be patient with other people who don't sign up as quickly as they did. This will probably happen with their *C* friend. The *C* type will study showing the Plan from every perspective and then do it again just to make sure they have everything right. The *C* will want to be technically correct and understand the proper procedure before sharing with someone else. This valuable opportunity and the most important benefits to the Independent Business Owner are so important to share with that prospect that the **C** doesn't have to anticipate every question. The odds are that the **C** will know the answers to most of the potential questions because they asked those questions themselves. Showing the Plan will build their confidence in their ability to do it right. They might learn from the **I** how valuable their own enthusiasm can be, for the **I** will enthusiastically tell everyone they can about this exciting new business! The **I** may, in turn, ask the **C** for more details about the business, so that the **I** can share more of the story with those people who seem to ask so many questions, and do not seem to believe the **I** at first...

Each personality style has their own special fears about showing the Plan, no matter how many times they have done it. This is a business of duplication, so whatever your fears might be as a new Independent Business Owner showing the Plan for the first time or as a veteran feeling stuck in a rut—your Sponsor and upline organization have a proven process for you to follow to achieve success. Their coaching will help you to:

- understand what makes this business work
- gain confidence and knowledge about the products
- list the people to whom you can present the opportunity
- learn how to Show the Plan effectively
- learn how to follow through to answer your prospects' questions
- learn how to get new IBOs started in the business by coaching them, based on their personality style, to do these same things
- practice adjusting to different personality styles to become successful in this process, over and over again...

Showing the Plan is a proven process, but understanding how your personality style affects your approach to showing the Plan is important as well. These personality insights will increase your effectiveness, your fun, your comfort level, and your accuracy as you successfully show the Plan!

THE PEOPLE

The third **P** is the People. The people in this business come from all walks of life, and you need to be able to relate to them individually so that you can successfully work with them. After one of our presentations to Emeralds and above, one Diamond made a very true statement, "It's *impossible* to be successful in this business if you don't understand people." The business world often places more importance on products and the plans they develop than on the people who make it happen. An unfortunate result of ignoring the people part of business is the repeated spending required to rehire and retrain, instead of an original wise investment in correct placement. Business management needs to understand that customer service is all about personality issues too. A study once showed that seven out of ten businesses stay in business less than ten years. In every instance, the primary reason for business failure was poor service. Understanding people so that you can be successful in this business doesn't have to be a trial and error process. Every Independent Business Owner can study personality styles in order to have better relationships and build better teams.

When you take a moment to compare your Personality Style Graphs to your spouse's or Sponsor's, you will see that they may be opposite, similar in some ways, but different in others. Each of us may have a different viewpoint and different responses because of our pace and our priority. One is not better than the other; they are just different. We all face a challenge to treat everyone the way they want and need to be treated. Naturally, we would treat everyone like *we* want to be treated. As we work with others according to their styles, we can build real teams where together everyone achieves more!

Let's look at a real life case study to gain insights into how this works. From the beginnings of Amway Corporation, this wonderful story shows people understanding and appreciating each other's differences. Two men whose personalities were not at all alike appreciated and worked together very effectively. Jay Van Andel has a lot of reserved, task-oriented traits, while Rich DeVos has a more outgoing, people-oriented style. In their autobiographies they share how they became friends in high school when Rich paid Jay twenty-five cents a week for a ride to school. In his autobiography, *An Enterprising Life*, Jay tells this story:

> Rich and I gradually got to know one another, and
> we became good friends. We double-dated together,
> went to basketball games together, had fun together,
> and talked about what we wanted to do with our
> lives. Rich was more gregarious than I was, more
> extroverted, always making a little more noise. I
> was more of a bookworm, quieter than Rich, but
> despite our differences I enjoyed his presence — it
> brought out the best in me. We found in time that
> our different personalities perfectly complemented
> one another, so that the two of us made an unbeat-
> able pair at whatever we set our minds to doing.
> By the time I graduated from high school in 1942,
> we knew that we were friends for life.

They knew they wanted to be business partners for life, too. Over the next few years, they operated a flying service, a drive-in hamburger stand, produced a wooden toy horse, developed a Nutrilite® supplement Distributorship... and then started the Amway Corporation.

Jay and Rich realized they were different, and that because of those differences they complemented each other well. As we learn about personality styles, we can acknowledge our personality differences and explore how we can complement each other like they did.

Rich and Jay not only accepted their differences, understood that they complemented each other, but even celebrated their differences! In difficult times, when neither man might have succeeded alone, the strength of their teamwork was the secret of their success:

> We persisted, however, continuing to advertise and
> hold meetings at the airport. We would show a film,
> then give a sales presentation, just as we did that
> first night. Rich then, as now, did most of the
> talking. I helped answer questions and tried to keep
> the cranky projector functioning...
>
> ...That night, two people showed up. It was terribly
> awkward giving a sales presentation to just two

people in a room with two hundred seats. We probably sounded a little less than enthusiastic. Late that night, we drove back to Grand Rapids. Disheartened, I asked Rich if he thought we should continue with Nutrilite®. "If we can't do any better than that with all the publicity we did, maybe we should just drop the whole thing." For a moment Rich hung his head. Then I saw a look of fierce determination come over his face. "Nonsense!" he said. "We can't quit just because we had one down night! We know that it can work! Besides, we already have some Distributors who look like they could blow the lid off the sales volume we're doing now." Chided, I turned my thoughts to planning our next meeting. This was the optimistic, tenacious Rich I knew, and it wasn't the first time he had encouraged me to persist when things began to look a little bad. In fact, if you're looking for "insider information" on how we became successful, you could start with two words: persistence and enthusiasm.

What have you learned about Rich and Jay?

Would you say that Jay is more outgoing or more reserved?

Circle one: Outgoing   Reserved

Would you say that Jay is more task or people oriented?

Circle one: Task   People

Putting these together, which of the four personality types do you think is strongest in Jay?

Circle one:

Would you say that Rich is more outgoing or more reserved?

Circle one: Outgoing   Reserved

Would you say that Rich is more task or people oriented?

Circle one: Task   People

Putting these together, which of the four personality types do you think is strongest in Rich?

Circle one: **D**   **I**   **S**   **C**

In Chapter Five, "Style at a Glance," you will learn some helpful methods for identifying a person's high style, or strongest personality type, like we just did for Rich and Jay. Jay described Rich as being "more gregarious," "extroverted," and "making a little more noise", which would indicate he has more of a high *I* style. Jay described himself as "more of a bookworm, quieter than Rich," who "tried to keep the cranky projector functioning." With this description, we can identify Jay as having more of a high *C* style.

Because these two men were able to work as a team, using their very different strengths, you know their names and they have affected your life. Look at the story of Jay and Rich and the drive home after the airport meeting. At the meeting, Rich used his *I* personality strengths to do most of the talking while Jay's *C* personality strengths were used to give quality answer to questions. After the poorly attended meeting, Jay was disheartened, and we see the struggle of a high *C* with a critical perspective. Jay said, "If we can't do any better than that ... maybe we should just drop the whole thing." Rich's optimistic high *I* style quickly came to the rescue saying, "Nonsense! ...We know that it can work! Besides, we already have some Distributors...!"

Jay also provides insight into how his high *C* style benefited the team:

> *As Amway expanded, Rich and I developed our own unique areas of expertise. Rich naturally took to motivational speaking and Distributor relations, while I began developing a facility with financial analysis and internal affairs. It's not as though we sat down and said, "OK, I'll take care of international expansion and you take care of research and development," and so on. It was more of an*

understanding that we had — we each understood where the strengths of the other lay, so we each made room for the other to use those strengths to his fullest potential. The specialization we worked out helped Amway run smoothly for decades.

THINKER

We love how Jay says that they "made room for the other to use those strengths"! This is just how one personality style benefits another and together everyone achieves more.

Did Rich and Jay understand *DISC* personality styles when they began their lifelong partnership so many years ago? Probably not, but they did understand that somehow they complemented each other, and they respected the differences that made their team work.

They first understood, then appreciated, and finally celebrated what they had learned to value: their different strengths. They effectively used that team strength to bring mutual success.

You may not be able to explain the force of gravity to us, but you don't have to understand all about gravity in order for it to affect you. Gravity happens, whether we understand it or not. Dr. Rohm also likes to say, "I don't understand how a brown cow eats green grass, then gives white milk that makes yellow butter – but I really like it!" Rich and Jay may not have known about *DISC* personality styles, but we can see that they understood how *their* personality styles worked together. That's why we say, "*DISC* is what happens!" — all the time, with all people, whether we understand it or not! Doesn't it make sense that if we can understand *DISC* personality styles, we can build more effective teams?

You gain a great advantage in life and business when you *DISC*over your own personality style and learn how your pace and perspective affect your own behavior. You will also increase your success with people when you can meet the unspoken needs and expectations of others. You can empower others to improve their success when you share this information with them to understand their "personality puzzles."

Consider this: Jay Van Andel and Rich DeVos could form an effective team for such great accomplishments because they understood their personality strengths and struggles. Understanding **DISC** personality styles can help you to gain this same skill with people. After all, if I understand you and you understand me, doesn't it make sense that we'll have a better relationship? You can empower your team so that everyone can accomplish their dreams!

CHAPTER ONE

PERSONAL ACTION PLAN

Question 1: Are you more comfortable working with the Products, the Plan or the People in the business? _____

_____

_____

Question 2: As this relates to your personality style, why do you think this is true? _____

_____

_____

_____

Question 3: The next time you present the Plan, observe which of the three **P**s your prospect seem to be most interested in.

_____

_____

_____

It's a People Business

According to Merrill Lynch, if we could shrink the Earth's population to a single village of exactly 100 people, with all existing human ratios remaining the same, it would look like this:

- There would be 57 Asians, 21 Europeans, 14 from the Western Hemisphere (including North, Central and South America) and 8 Africans.

- 51 would be female; 49 would be male.

- 70 would be nonwhite; 30 would be white.

- 70 would be non-Christian; 30 would be culturally Christian.

- Half of the entire world's wealth would be in the hands of only 6 people, and all 6 would be citizens of the United States of America.

- 80 would live in substandard housing.

- 70 would be unable to read in any language.

- 50 would suffer from malnutrition.

- 20 would be in poor health or diseased.

- One would be near death; one would be near birth.

- Only one would have a college education.

- No one would own a computer.

Such a village would be full of very different people. When we consider our world from such an incredibly compressed perspective, we feel just how much we need to learn to function together with compassion and understanding.

God must enjoy diversity to have made us so different! Think for a moment about all the different shapes, sizes, colors, and scents of all the flowers in the entire world. And what about insects? Could anyone remember how many different insects there are? There are over six hundred kinds of beetles alone! The place that each of us calls *home* is special to share because of the unique complexity it displays in its people, terrain, vegetation, animals, weather, and the list could go on...

God has made this kind of diversity in people, and people in the business are just as diverse. These millions of people from all over the world come from all walks of life. They come in different sizes, shapes, and packaging. Why are they so different? "We don't choose these people," Van Andel once said. "They choose themselves. In Amway, everyone is a volunteer. And when people volunteer, you get all different kinds of people. That's the way we want it to be."

Diversity enriches us all, but if we want to learn to function together with compassion and understanding, we must be able to find common ground on which to stand. We need common ground on which to build strong businesses.

Where can we find common ground? If we look at personality styles, can we begin to understand many different people? Crossing all cultural, ethnic, religious, or any other boundaries, what personality styles do we see? Looking at that same village we looked at beginning the chapter, we would find these personality styles:

- 10 people who have a high *D* type personality style.
- 30 people who have a high *I* type personality style.
- 35 people who have a high *S* type personality style.
- 25 people who have a high *C* type personality style.

DISC reduces something very complex, individual behavior, to something simple by starting with just four behavioral types. In every culture studied, **DISC** styles of behavior have been validated. Even though our world village is so diverse, we can begin to understand each other from this perspective. It allows us to *see* people beyond their outward appearance. We may be different in sex, race, nationality, size or shape, but we find common ground by identifying and understanding our common personality styles. **DISC** helps us recognize our perspectives, motivations, and needs. We find common ground to connect with others on a deeper level. It encourages us to accept them for who they are... and who they can be. It helps us learn how to better work with each individual person.

Lee Iacocca brought Chrysler Corporation back from inferior workmanship, labor disputes and bankruptcy, because he knew that business must succeed *most* at the people level. He insisted, "In the end, all business operations can be reduced to three words: people, product, and profits. People come first."

At the turn of the last century, a business magnate wrote, "Down in their hearts, wise men know this truth: The only way to help yourself is to help others." In this business, you will succeed best by understanding people and coaching them toward fulfilling their dreams. As one movie buff said, "Our business plays on the wide screen. The one common part each actor plays, in the movie, is that they have a dream." As you understand your personality style and the other person's style, you can adapt to really communicate with them. By recognizing their potential, giving them the tools to develop their abilities, and helping them to improve their lives and reach their dreams, you will succeed in reaching your dreams!

Zig Ziglar says,

> *Money isn't everything, but it ranks pretty close to oxygen!*

Making money is important to people no matter what their dreams are. They want to use money to gain control of their time... or to give their children the things they need... or to travel and experience all the diversity in our world... or to have influence with influential people... All these dreams require some amount of money. Money is a necessary part of our lives, and people get into this business to make money, but they really want money to use it to fulfill their dreams.

How can this business help people to realize their dreams? On the surface, your business shares some common elements with traditional business: goods and services are moved through a distribution channel to consumers; profitability is determined by volume; marketing techniques make potential customers aware; customer satisfaction is essential. Beneath the surface, however, your Independent Business Ownership is very different: you do not have a retail store; you have minimal overhead and inventory; you do not deal with employment issues, such as hiring, firing and work schedules; you work for yourself, so you set your own schedule and productivity goals.

In this business, the biggest difference is YOU.

This business stretches you, commits you, scares you, challenges you, excites you, changes you. In a way, it's all about you. Understanding your personality style can help you as you grow with your business. In another way, it's not about you—it's about the people in your upline who care about your success, and those in your downline for whom you care. It really is true that "You are in business *for* yourself, but not *by* yourself." As you grow with your business, you will interact with more people who probably will be increasingly different from you. The people skills you will need to build relationships with many different individuals will be critical for your success in this business. Using relationship marketing will be vital.

RELATIONSHIP MARKETING

What is relationship marketing? When our editor Julie was first introduced to the business, she was skeptical of this concept.

Julie explains,

When I first learned about relationship marketing, I thought it was a nice way to avoid the fact that somebody has to sell products for this business to work. I didn't understand that the real issue in any retail operation is not selling, but buying. Money is not made when the seller sells, but when the buyer buys!

We were interested in the business, so I bought some SA8 and tried it. And I kept thinking. Why had I always previously bought laundry detergent at the local store? I had used my [brand X] laundry detergent for years. I knew what it cost and what I could expect from it. I knew how long it would last and where to get more. I was used to going to that particular aisle and shelf at my local store. That was a comfortable habit for me. It was simple. I am a busy mother of four with a demanding career. What would motivate me to change this habit?

I recognized two important things. First, I understood how this business could work for me and how it could help me fulfill my dreams. I was willing to change my buying habits to fulfill my dreams. Second, my relationship with my upline and my trust in their recommendations made me want to try a new product. If I liked that product – and I really did – I was motivated to rearrange my habits to accommodate this change. Then I found myself wondering if my upline had tried the vitamins...

This thought surprised me. I began to see why relationship marketing really works. It was my relationship with my upline that made me want to listen. When I listened I began to understand how the business could help me fulfill my dreams. Then I was really motivated to make changes in my buying habits. And this motivation is the first step in building a business.

How important was Julie's relationship with her upline? Her upline built her confidence in the value and quality of SA8®. Her upline built a bridge between her and this business. This relationship is the key to this business! Zig Ziglar says, "If people like you, they will spend time with you, but if they trust you, they will do business with you." This book is about understanding yourself and others, because building relationships is foundational in building a successful business.

Remember,

"Products don't move people; people move products."

Many successful businesses spend millions of advertising dollars to give us perceived relationships. They want us to buy products from...

- Wendy's – you know her dad, Dave, makes the best hamburgers
- Disney – a man with a mouse and a dream
- McDonald's – Ronald makes a kid's mealtime fun
- Wal-Mart Stores – Sam Walton lived the American Dream for us
- Orville Reddenbacher – the name means popcorn
- Chrysler – Lee Iacocca made us all believe in our Detroit again
- Jello – Bill Cosby showed us how eating it is fun

Advertisers know that we will buy from someone with whom we can identify. Sam Walton was a regular guy who gave us a good deal, so we made him one of the richest men in the world. Advertisers also know that we will buy something because it gives us a perceived relationship with a person we admire. What does Michael Jordan know about making tennis shoes? Michael Jordan sells sports shoes because he is a hero to many kids. They love to wear his shoes. Even this kind of relationship marketing is effective.

 Relationship marketing is about understanding people and building quality relationships with others. Building quality relationships takes not only time, but it takes people skills too. Personality insights are the tools you need to develop the people skills that will help you as you develop the relationships that will build your business.

It is wonderful to meet new people and begin to form new relationships. A healthy, growing relationship takes an investment of your time to honestly understand and build trust with another person. You cannot become best friends with everyone, so the level of the relationship you form will be different with each person. Something as simple as your age or your children's ages can affect the depth of a relationship.

Your interests may draw you together naturally, or you may need to use these personality insights to recognize common ground for your relationship. Your business may become the common point of your relationship, but you need another starting point to build trust with them so that you can introduce them to the business. No matter what level of personal relationship develops, building an effective relationship for your business will require growing people skills. Using personality insights can help your people skills grow.

You already use people skills every day, because we all like doing business with people with whom we have developed some relationship. We like to eat dinner at the restaurant where the waitress knows what we like, or at a restaurant where we know the cook. We like to have our car worked on by the mechanic whom we trust. We will continue to do business with people with whom we have a satisfactory relationship.

Merck and Company discovered that replacing a worker who resigned or was discharged cost one and one-half times that worker's yearly salary. After finding a replacement worker, the next issue was how the new person would *fit* in the corporate culture of that business. In this business, you spend time, effort and money contacting prospects, showing the Plan to them, following up, getting them started, showing the Plan for them, training them, answering their questions, building depth... How much is it worth for them to decide they *fit* in the business? It is a big investment of your time, effort and money. Every Independent Business Owner faces the challenge of maintaining effective business relationships. Let's explore how some traditional businesses face this challenge.

According to Maxwell's *Be a People Person*, most customers won't complain to a store's management if something goes wrong with their purchase. Depending on the customer's perception of the severity of the problem, the customer will tell between nine and 16 others about their bad experience — and 13% will tell more than 20! More than two out of three customers who receive poor service will never buy from that store again — and management will never know why!

Think about it. What happened? The first thing we see is that something went wrong when the purchase did not meet the expectations of the customer. and the customer wants the store to do something to meet their expectations. Now the relationship between the customer and the store will be affected. Any relationship is based upon the expectation that both parties will contribute something of value to the other. Poor customer service means that the store salesperson did not do what was needed to satisfy the expectations of the customer.

Not only did the salesperson leave the customer dissatisfied, but the customer left the store with the perception that the store was not interested in meeting their expectations. Telling others about the bad experience will warn others that the store does not really make an effort to satisfy the customer's expectations and will thus take advantage of them too.

Store management never has the chance to be involved, because the customer's initial relationship with the salesperson has not been successful in satisfying the customer's expectations, either from the product or from the manner in which the salesperson has dealt with them. If only the store salesperson had shown a personal interest in meeting the needs of the customer, that relationship could have won the customer back for the store.

TAKE ACTION When someone has a problem, the first thing they naturally do is to go to the person in the situation with whom they have a good relationship, who is also in a position to help them with the problem.

We feel that this person has satisfactorily met our expectations in the past, so they may be able to help us with this problem too. This is a secret in relationships that we often forget. How do we understand the other person's true expectations, so that we can try to satisfy *them*? This requires insight into another personality, into understanding their needs. This is how we build good relationships, so that when problems arise, the other person will feel the freedom to come to us, instead of feeling that the best solution is severing the relationship.

As we have shared the concepts of personality styles with hundreds of people, we have seen problems, conflicts, disagreements or wrongs inevitably occur in relationships. The relationships that will survive these difficulties that inevitably arise, are relationships in which both people communicate mutual respect and contribute something of value to the other person. This is true in friendship, family, romance, marriage or business relationships.

These concepts are vital to relationship marketing. Personality insights help us communicate mutual respect and recognize the valuable contribution that someone wants and needs from us. This is the foundation for a lasting relationship that can be formed both upline and downline and will keep people in the business. A friend, who is a Marine, has often shared with us that there is no such thing as an *ex-Marine*. He insists, "Once a Marine, always a Marine!" Why is this so true? Marines honor the relationships that shaped their values and thoughts and made them permanent members of that select group. The valuable contribution they have made to one another is so great that denying this association would be denying part of themselves. We all rest easier at night knowing that they are willing to lock arms together for a common goal—and depend on those relationships that help them protect our freedom. We need this kind of relationships in our business.

We all make mistakes in our relationships, and in business relationships too. Can we successfully resolve conflicts and stay in business relationships? We can do this if we can learn to recognize missed expectations and reach agreement about how to satisfy both parties involved. The Technical Assistance Research Programs Report on dissatisfied customers showed that 95% of dissatisfied customers will buy from the store again if their problems are resolved. Even better, they will each tell eight people about the resolution. What's the secret in turning the situation around? Simply this: they feel that somebody cared!

How did they care? When the customer tells a salesperson about the problem, the salesperson must listen for the customer's expectations that were not met. If the salesperson can meet these expectations, he must do so. If he cannot, he must communicate respect for the customer and explain what he can do that will meet the expectations of the customer in a way that is also acceptable to the store. If this solution is agreeable to the customer, the salesperson has preserved the relationship successfully. If this solution is not agreeable, the salesperson can communicate that the manager will care for the customer, and that the manager has the authority to offer another solution. The manager can step in to use the same process to resolve the problem with the customer.

This process is so much easier when the salesperson or the manager understands **DISC**. If they understand **DISC**, they will understand their own communication style. They will recognize the customer's personality style and have some clues to the customer's expectations. They will know that a **D** wants choices and options to resolve problems or that a **C** wants quality answers to questions. They will know that the **S** must be very upset to come to them at all, because harmony is very important to them. They will recognize that the **I** wants to know everyone likes them so they may forget to express their problem at all. They will adjust what they say to the customer so that they will communicate according to these expectations. These basic insights can mean the difference between resolving an issue and severing a relationship.

Look forward to Chapter Ten, "Styles at a Glance," to learn how you, too, can recognize how to communicate with someone according to their personality style expectations.

Does this sound too simple, too basic? Vince Lombardi won many football games because he stuck to the basics. Mother Teresa simply focused on helping others in need. You can build a successful business using these relationship basics.

Relationship marketing is building relationships that will market our products, build our business, and realize our dreams. In any relationship, we will encounter issues that must be resolved successfully without severing the relationship. Personality insights empower us to understand ourselves and others so we can communicate mutual respect and understand our expectations so that we can satisfactorily meet our needs. In this way, we will build good relationships for personal loyalty within our business.

People that you bring into the business will want to grow in it as your relationship with them grows. Personality insights can help your relationships grow and help you resolve the conflicts that inevitably arise. Dr. Paul Tournier wrote: "He who feels loved, feels understood, and he who feels understood, feels loved." If you want to succeed in a people business, you must succeed in understanding people. That's what this book is all about.

Right now someone you know has this kind of relationship with you. They will hear you present the Plan because they know you and trust you to share something of value to them. What are you waiting for?

A TAKE ACTION

CHAPTER TWO

PERSONAL ACTION PLAN

Question 1: In almost any business interaction, whether at a hotel, a restaurant, or even a gas station, it seems that a product or a task causes the difficulties. However, the real problem is caused by how a person handles the difficulty. Out of your experience, give an example where you have observed this to be true?

_____

_____

_____

_____

Question 2: What situation are you currently involved in, where you find yourself focusing more on the task at hand, rather than the relationship with the people involved?

_____

_____

_____

_____

_____

_____

What's your PQ?

At an early age, Dr. Rohm remembers being in school and hearing about something called *IQ*. He did not know what it meant, but he knew that it was important. Parents, as well as teachers, put a lot of emphasis on your *IQ*. Some people were even placed in certain groups at school based on their *IQ*.

Do you remember learning about your *IQ*? As children, we did not know how you got it, nor what to do to make it better, but we knew that "being smart" played a very important role in your school life. As adults, these things make more sense. Your *IQ* is important. We now understand that *IQ*, your Intelligence Quotient, measures how quickly we learn, but not how much we can learn. We also know that a high *IQ* alone does not guarantee success in life.

Several excellent articles and books have been written about other key ingredients to success in life. Have you heard about *EQ*? This is your Emotional Quotient, your ability to recognize how you and those around you are feeling, as well as the ability to generate, understand, and regulate emotions. Scientific research shows that different parts of the brain have different purposes, and that emotional responses come from specific areas of the brain. The information is all quite technical, and it shows that emotional intelligence is separate from other kinds of intelligence. We commonly call it intuition, instinct, or a "gut feeling." *EQ* is a basis for judgment when we choose something because we like it, or it just feels right. As you can well imagine, the high *I* and *S* personality styles will generally have a higher *EQ*, because of sensitivity to other people's emotions, than the high *D* and *C* styles, who tend to focus more on tasks. Studies show that your *EQ* is an important factor in your success in life.

What about your *AQ*? Your Adversity Quotient measures your ability to respond effectively to adversity. Factors influencing your *AQ* are control, ownership, effect and endurance. You may easily understand areas over which you can exercise control, doing what you effectively can do when you encounter adversity. You may, on the other hand, spend much emotional energy worrying about areas over which you have little or no control. A second factor in your Adversity Quotient is your ability to take ownership of your part in the problem and its solution. Taking ownership in your part, while leaving the responsibility of others with them, allows you to spend your energy working out a good solution for your part. If you take ownership for the parts of the problem that really are not yours, you will probably be very frustrated by the limitations on what you can do and may miss taking care of your part. Simply stated, you cannot control other people, but you can control yourself. The **D** and **C** personality styles, with their task orientation, will usually be quick to exercise control and take their ownership of a problem.

Understanding your personality style and staying under control are key factors in the third factor in your Adversity Quotient. The third factor, limiting the effects of a crisis to appropriate areas in your life, will keep you from making the problem bigger than it really is. Each **DISC** type has a different struggle in this area. Knowing that your endurance is stronger than the problem is the last factor in your **AQ**. Each **DISC** type has traits that help and hinder endurance. Knowing you can endure and then choosing to do it is an important part of your Adversity Quotient. The **D** and **S** styles will usually endure, the **D** because of their tenacity and the **S** because of their steadiness. The **I** relies on their optimism and the strength of others to endure. The **C** endures because they anticipated the adversity and expected to deal with it in the first place! How you deal with the adversity that we all encounter in life is so important to your success.

We will address emotions and explore response to adversity further in our upcoming book, *The Facets of Life.*

Look for it!

May we introduce you to what we believe is perhaps the most important "quotient" in your life? Your **PQ**, or *Personality Quotient*, is your ability to understand yourself and others for effective communication and teamwork. Unless you live alone on an island, you will have contact with other people: family members, fellow workers, church family, friends, neighbors, and most importantly for this book, your business associates. Your success in life will depend in many ways on your **PQ**. If you only understand life from your own perspective, which is the most *natural* way to view things, you will often fail to communicate and work effectively with others. We need to learn to see things from another personality perspective, which is a *supernatural* way to view things. In this supernatural way, we can see both sides of a story, or many aspects of a situation. We can really see the bigger picture!

FOUR STEPS

There are four important steps to raising your **PQ**. The first step is understanding yourself, especially your personality style. Understanding your personality style helps you to see what you do more objectively, as you begin to focus on your perspective from the patterns in your behavior. Understanding another person, and how their perspective may be different from yours, is the second step. Simply being able to focus on their perspective objectively, outside your own frame of reference, is such an enlightening experience. You may be truly able to see life through their eyes for the first time! The third step, adapting your style to have better relationships, enables you to adapt your words and actions toward another person so that you communicate effectively with them, according to their personality style rather than your own, so that you speak from their perspective instead of yours. This is the key to building a better relationship. The fourth step expands the scope of your effective communication to include a group of people who function as a team. You will recognize and appreciate the strengths and struggles of each person on the team. Drawing on the strengths of each personality style allows you to form effective teams because you begin to recognize that *all* of us is better than *one* of us! We will continue to grow individually as we grow together.

These four steps open new areas of effective communication and teamwork – they empower you to raise your **PQ** !

Four Steps to Raising your *PQ*

1. Understanding yourself through your personality style

2. Understanding another person through their personality style

3. Adapting your style to have better relationships

4. Building better teams where *Together Everyone Achieves More!*

Step One
Understanding Yourself

The first step is understanding yourself. Although it is not required for you to do a personality profile assessment before you are able to proceed in this book, the material will become more meaningful for you when you do an assessment. See the Appendix for further details. Even if you have not completed an assessment, you will probably identify most with one of the statements from each of the following perspective discussions.

If you have completed an assessment, take a moment to review the Appendix at this time. Look at your Basic Style, which is Graph II. Looking at the **DISC** type that is highest in your style, along with the other types(s) above the midline, can show you many things. The statements corresponding to the highest **DISC** type in your personality style should answer questions like these: *What is your Outlook on Life – what really makes you tick? What is your focus in problem solving? What environment is ideal for you to feel comfortable, so that you can do your best work?* For example, Dr. Rohm has a very high **I**. He is very outgoing and very people-oriented. He likes to persuade others to his way of thinking and focuses on having fun together in the process! He likes an environment that is friendly, fun and exciting! Stewart has a very high

D, so he likes to be in charge of projects where he can focus on getting things done. He likes an environment that is upbeat, fast and powerful.

Think carefully about your style as you read the charts that follow. Take a moment to highlight or circle the statements that you feel apply to you.

A TAKE
C
T
I
O
N

Outlook on Life

D ...... likes to lead or be in charge

I .... likes to persuade others to their way of thinking

S ...... likes to provide necessary support to help complete the job

C .... likes consistent quality and excellence

How does your outlook on life affect what you do? It is your starting point, the perspective from which you look at any situation in life. When our Personality Insights team began to work on this book, look at how our difference of outlook shows: Stewart, who has a high **D**, took charge of the project right away and decided what we needed to do, and who would do what. Dr. Rohm, with his high **I**, told us some good stories to inspire us with the significance of the project. These stories would give life to the book. Julie, who has a high **D** and **C**, wanted to know just what part of the project would be hers and shared her ideas for quality material that would give substance to the book. Nancy, our administrative assistant who has a high **S**, offered to provide her support by typing materials for the book. We each approached our project from a different perspective because of our difference of outlook on life, and this difference is the strength of our team! In the same way, your outlook on life gives you a special approach to everything you do.

Focus

D .... Get the job done—just do it! Overcome opposition and achieve your goals! Winners never quit and quitters never win!

I ....I am for you! We can have fun, and if we all pull in the same direction, our success will never end!

S ....All for one and one for all! If we all work together we make a great team. All of us is better than one of us.

C ....Anything worth doing is worth doing correctly. Provide quality goods and services through careful and conscientious work.

Focus comes into play when we encounter problems. What do we focus on when a problem arises? Looking at the list above, we can see what a difference this creates! Do you just push ahead, or look to the group for a tension-breaking laugh? Do you sit back and figure out the correct way to do something, or do you look for ways that you can help someone in the group so that the project can be completed? One of these will be your main focus as you encounter problems.

Your secondary type(s) above the midline will play a secondary role as you focus on solving your problem. Julie has a style blend having a high **D** and secondary **C**. Her focus will be to find the *correct* solution so that she then can get the job *done*. She doesn't want to have to come back and fix another problem created by a too hasty solution. The secondary type in her style serves the highest type as she focuses on getting the job done, while doing it correctly. As you can imagine , she often struggles with how perfectly something can be done and still be able to get it *done*! Chapter Four, "Basic Building Styles," will further explain this concept.

Our environment always affects us. It may make it harder for us to concentrate or communicate, while a change of environment may make those things easier. Each of us has an ideal environment, where we are most comfortable and most easily able to relate, communicate, and accomplish our best work. Defining your ideal environment can be so vital to creating the environment you need, instead of waiting for it to happen by chance.

Their Ideal Environment

D ....Upbeat, fast, powerful

I ....Fun, friendly, exciting

S ....Predictable, stable, harmonious

C ....Structure with procedures, accuracy, quality

Your Ideal Environment is the situation that you like best, one in which you can relax and relate to people, and feel invigorated to do your best work. Would it be safe to say that an ideal environment for a **C** type, with structure for procedures, accuracy, and quality, would be a stressful environment for an **I** type who wants an environment that is fun, friendly, and exciting? Remember how Dr. Rohm says that opposites attract? People who have different styles often marry and then go into the business together. As opposites, they attract, then they attack! They really need to understand their differences in ideal environment! Think about a time when you did your best work. You will probably find that this situation created an ideal environment for you to interact and perform.

Their Basic Need

D ....Challenge, control, choice

I ....Recognition, approval, popularity

S ....Appreciation, security, affirmation

C ....Quality answers, value, excellence

Dr. Rohm loves to say that people don't do things *against you* – they do things *for themselves*! Each of us naturally seeks to meet our own basic needs. Sometimes, these needs are easily met, but often we search for ways to meet them. Understanding our own basic needs can help us see what may have prompted us to do something that another may misunderstand. How different is a **D** type, who needs challenge and control, from an **S** type, who needs security and appreciation!

Julie likes to say that *we* give people what *we* need, not what *they* need. When a person who has a high **I** style and needs recognition and approval tells a person with a high **C** style to stand up and take a bow in front of the group, can you see that this doesn't meet the need of the person who has a high **C**? The same thing happens when the person with a high **C** gives a detailed analysis of the quality of a product to a person with a high **I**! Giving the other person what they need really satisfies them, so it will really satisfy us. To do this, we must first understand what *we* need and then what *they* need.

In all of these ways, **DISC** personality types deal with life from a different perspective *every day*! You can begin to understand yourself better as you reread the previous statements that you chose to describe yourself.

As you continue to read **Sponsor with Style**, take time to make the information yours by highlighting **DISC** insights that apply especially to you. Notice how your outlook on life shows in your approach. Begin to be aware of your focus and how people respond to you in everyday situations, especially as problems arise. Recognize how you respond when your ideal environment is created. Think about your decision-making processes, and explore what needs you meet as you make decisions. This is all part of Step One, Understanding Yourself.

STEP TWO
UNDERSTANDING OTHERS

The second step in raising your **PQ** is to take what you have learned about yourself and expand your insights to include another person. Your spouse, your friend, your co-worker, or the person you have just sponsored probably has a personality style that is different from yours. You can begin to explore how their personality style may make their perspective, their attitudes, and their preferences different from yours. They may see life from a very different perspective from yours. Look back at the descriptions above, and take note of the *Outlook on Life, Focus, Ideal Environment and Basic Needs* that you did not choose as your own. These will describe a very different perspective than your choices describe! For example, when Julie talks to Dr. Rohm about a work project, she remembers that her focus will be to get the job done (high **D**), but his focus will be having fun (high **I**) while doing it! Chapter Five, *Styles at a Glance*, will give you some practical tips for identifying another person's basic style so that you will know where to begin as you understand another person.

Your spouse or a close friend may also be willing to show you their Basic Style, which is Graph II from the Adult Profile Assessment or their personalized computer report. When you know the high type(s) in their style, you can refer to these charts for insights into their *Outlook, Focus, Ideal Environment* and *Basic Needs*. You will begin to understand how their perspective is like yours, or how they may be different from you. You will begin to understand that how they behave and how they express something is often a result of their personality perspective. You will then *see* through their eyes and be able to understand them better. This is the beginning of Step Two – Understanding Others.

STEP THREE
ADAPTING YOUR STYLE TO HAVE BETTER RELATIONSHIPS

As you understand another person better, you will begin to see the differences between you in a different light. Step Three – *Adapting Your Style to Have Better Relationships* means exercising your ability to communicate effectively and act intelligently by adapting your words and actions to their style so that you can meet their needs. Now that's a mouthful! Simply put, this means that instead of giving someone else what *you* need, you give them what *they* need – in order to truly communicate!

How do Dr. Rohm and Julie do this? When Julie meets with Dr. Rohm to work on a project, she remembers to allow him some time to talk about their project, because recognition and approval are his basic needs. She recognizes him by listening to him, and carefully approves anything he says on which she can agree. Because she needs choices, he often asks her questions about how she might like to work on the project. Giving her choices helps her communicate her ideas on the project. They make room for the needs of the other person, so that each is comfortable, open to communicate and work together. This sounds so polite, and it is!

Adapting their styles is even more important when they feel the other person is doing something *just* to drive them crazy! It requires understanding their different personality styles and exercising more self-control through intelligent choices. They have to *think* before they *act*! When Julie is *driving* (high **D**) to get the wording on a project consistently *correct* (she has a high **C** too!), Dr. Rohm may feel like telling a *funny* story to lighten the mood (high **I**), but he doesn't. He takes a deep breath and comes up with another *choice* for wording that they both feel is *correct*. He makes room for her *drive* for *correctness* because he respects her ability to produce *concise clarity*. Sometimes Dr. Rohm gets distracted from getting to a project, but Julie doesn't get irritated and begin to push him (high **D**), because she chooses to remember that he (a high **I**) sometimes gets sidetracked telling stories or talking to a friend at lunch. She finds another project to work on until he returns. She makes room for his storytelling, knowing that the same storytelling is what makes their products highly effective because they are so much fun!

Recognizing that the perspective that is opposite yours is valuable is the real basis for Step Three. If you are Task-oriented, find value in people. If you are People-oriented, remember how important it really is to complete your tasks. Watch for the good that comes when an Outgoing person reaches out to you, or see how important a Reserved manner is when uncovering and correcting mistakes. Adapting your style to have better relationships will be easier when you can really value, understand and appreciate a perspective that is different from your own.

Closing in on Step Three

Here is a recent example of how *Adapting your Style to Have Better Relationships* works in real life...

After seeing the *Sponsor with Style* Seminar at his own function, one Diamond focused on learning to adapt his style to be more effective with his IBOs. This gentle Diamond has a high *S* style. These personality insights helped him understand that his *own* basic need for security and appreciation caused him to use verbal affirmation to give *others* security and appreciation. He would come alongside his leaders individually and let them know that he appreciated them and would always be there to do anything he could do to help them. Awakening to the fact that he was giving them what *he* needed, he wanted to adapt his style to better meet the needs of each of his leaders. He wanted to give them what *they* needed. For a number of years, he had tried to coach one of his leaders, a very high *D*, but they always seemed to stop short of effective communication. His style worked well with others, but it just didn't connect with this particular IBO. Could he adapt to the style of this IBO?

In the past, when they approached a problem, the Diamond would listen; his IBO would state the problem and then declare a solution, deciding how they should fix it. The IBO wanted to act immediately, but the Diamond was so stressed that he simply did not know what to do or say. This time, he tried something new. When they reached their old familiar impasse, the Diamond was really stressed, but recognized that this stress was caused by his *own* need for harmony and stability. When the IBO wanted to rush out and fix this problem, the Diamond felt his emotions climbing higher again. Then the Diamond realized that he was creating his own stress — it wasn't the IBO who was upset. After all, the IBO actually *liked* the challenge of fixing the problem! The Diamond saw that he was really only upsetting himself. He was uncomfortable with the powerful approach of the high *D*.

How did he see this? He remembered his style wanted affirmation before action, the time to think about how this might affect harmony and stability for everyone involved. He recognized that this IBO had a high *D* style, so the IBO wanted to make choices, to be fast and powerful as he sought to get results. What a difference in their approach! Just remembering this difference in their perspectives helped the Diamond not to react negatively, because he realized that the IBO would naturally try to powerfully act on the problem. The Diamond saw that, in reality, his IBO really wanted to solve the problem, not just upset the Diamond's stability! Now the Diamond could relax and think so that he was able to offer good choices to the IBO. In this way he could help the IBO be successful in meeting the challenges that he was so eager to address. Successful communication at last! The high *D* IBO was invigorated to conquer the next challenge, and they both knew that the Diamond was ready, willing and able to help him to accomplish this goal!

This Diamond was so excited to share his success story with us! He couldn't wait for another chance to adapt his style for this kind of real communication. His business would benefit, and the relationship that he enjoyed with this IBO was better than ever. As you begin to understand yourself, seek to understand another person through their personality style, and learn to adapt your style to have a better relationship, you will experience this for yourself too!

STEP FOUR
BUILDING BETTER TEAMS WHERE
TOGETHER EVERYONE ACHIEVES MORE!

When you are able to adapt your style to have a better relationship with another person, you are ready to begin Step Four – Building better teams where *Together Everyone Achieves More!* Each personality type has strengths and struggles. Your personality style has a unique blend that includes some strengths and some struggles from each type in your style. Building a *DISC* team means including the strengths of each *DISC* type on your team.

What makes a real team? A real team is not a group of people who work in the same business or do the same job. It is not a tag team, where one person does one part, passes the project to the next person who does their part, who then passes the project to the next person, and so on until the project is completed.

> A true team is a group of people who do something together through their interaction that no one on the team could do so well alone.

Powerful IDEA

This teamwork happens in families, workgroups, businesses, and especially in marriages. With true teamwork, the sum is greater than the parts alone or combined. Each member of the team is empowered to contribute from their special perspective, so that the chemistry of the team interaction creates magnified results. When you are part of a team, the results are exciting to see!

Can we **DISC**over what each type brings to the team?

D
Provides ADVENTURE
Brings DETERMINATION
Uses CREATIVITY
Stresses INNOVATION

I
Provides IMAGINATION
Brings SPONTANEITY
Uses INSPIRATION
Stresses INTERACTION

TOGETHER
EVERYONE
ACHIEVES
MORE!

C
Provides ANALYSIS
Brings LOGIC
Uses OBJECTIVITY
Stresses CONSISTENCY

S
Provides STABILITY
Brings HARMONY
Uses COMPATIBILITY
Stresses SECURITY

This book is a team effort. Stewart (high **D**) understands what needs to be included in the book so that it will speak to the issues of the business. Julie (high **D/C**) interacts with him using specific information about personality styles and technical writing issues so that together they create useful information about personality styles and the business. Dr. Rohm (high **I**) interacts with them and gives life to the information through his engaging presentation style and his ability to add interesting stories that expand our ability to relate to the information. Carol (high **S/C**) interacts with them to present this vital information on paper so you can enjoy reading and graphically understand it. Together, our team creates a book that you can read and understand and use effectively!

Your business requires teamwork. If you are married, you and your spouse function as a team in building your business. Understanding the roles that you each most effectively play is important. Do you have a high **I** style? You may then be the one to contribute most to your contact list. Do you have a high **C** style? You may contribute most by explaining and working with the details of placing orders. Do you have a high **D** style? You will want to drive your business to increasing levels of achievement. Do you have a high **S** style? You may contribute to the team through supporting individuals as they learn the System. When each one contributes from their strengths, the team benefits and the team really works.

What makes teamwork really *happen*? We must understand the value and role of each person on the team, and support the importance of their contribution. Stability (high **S**) and Creativity (high **D**) are very different, but both are very important contributions. We must interact in an environment that is conducive to open communication with each member. This means that we must be able to allow the person who has a high **I** style to make our interaction fun, while we maintain respect for rules for the person who has a high **C** style. Individual needs must be respected so that barriers of self-protection do not restrict inter-action. We must value the drive of the person with a high **D** style, without missing the balancing value of the routine of the person with a high **S** style. We must be able to question any idea without discounting the idea or the person who offered it. We must continue to interact until we find an idea with its correct expression which we, as a team, can embrace.

This teamwork takes practice, but being part of a team and its results are so exciting that they are worth the extra effort! As we are individually more effective in the first three steps, we are better equipped to build better teams. As we understand and appreciate the special strengths of different types, we can anticipate that people with certain high types in their styles will make their special contributions to our teams.

Raising your **IQ** may be somewhat of an impossible task. But raising your **PQ** just takes practice, and now you can do it! It will enrich your life, relationships, and your business!

Keep these four steps in mind as you read the rest of this book, and use them to effectively practice the insights you will learn:

FOUR STEPS TO RAISING YOUR *PQ*

 1. Understanding yourself through your personality style

 2. Understanding another person through their personality style

 3. Adapting your style to have better relationships

4. Building better teams where *Together Everyone Achieves More!*

CHAPTER THREE
PERSONAL ACTION PLAN

Step 1 – Understanding Yourself

Looking at your personality style, how would you list the **DISC** types in your style from highest, first, to lowest, last? You may refer to your Basic Style, Graph II, in Appendix A, or simply give a self-evaluation.

DISC types in My Style

1. _____

2. _____

3. _____

4. _____

Step 2 – Understanding Another Person

Looking at your spouse or closest friend, how would you list the types in their style from highest, first, to lowest, last?

DISC types in Their Style (Name: _____)

1. _____

2. _____

3. _____

4. _____

Step 3 – Adapting Your Style to Have Better Relationships

Review the charts on pp. 55-57. Looking at your highest type and considering this person's highest type (from question 2), what can you specifically adjust in your own style in order to have a better relationship with them?

_____

_____

_____

_____

_____

Step 4 – Building Better Teams

Looking at the Team Chart on page 63, what strengths do you and this person offer to your team?

_____

_____

_____

_____

_____

_____

_____

CHAPTER FOUR

Introduction to Business Building Styles

In this chapter we will begin with **PQ** Step One, *Understanding Yourself*, to begin exploring how your personality style builds the business. Each of us started with a dream and decided that this business was the vehicle to achieve it. With this vision for your dream, keeping in mind your past life and business experiences, you began the Independent Business Owner's adventure. Recognizing that your past experience may or may not prove helpful, you studied the facts about the business. Now you can learn the way that your unique personality style affects your approach to getting the business started and making it grow. Each personality style has its own characteristic strengths and struggles in business and a unique perspective and problem solving method. Your success in the business is enhanced when you understand your personality style and how it affects your business.

If you are a new Independent Business Owner, you will learn how your personality style influences the way you address the business. For the more experienced Independent Business Owner, this will be a fun look back at how your personality influenced your start in the business. You may also find it helpful in guiding your new Independent Business Owners to a good start in the business. This chapter will remind us that all Independent Business Owners have a personality perspective, and as we **DISC**over them, we begin Step Two, *Understanding Another Person*. We will be able to better coach and encourage them. We may even be able to predict or prevent some problems before they occur.

For your review, the diagram on the following page indicates how the four **DISC** types tend to view life in general. Think about how each type may set their goals and view their roles in building their business.

How do personality styles affect your approach to the business? Let's begin with a simple example which you may have experienced yourself... One of your first questions when you start in the business is

Dominant   **Inspiring**
Direct   **Influencing**
Demanding   **Impressionable**
Decisive   **Interactive**
Determined   **Impressive**
Doer   **Involved**

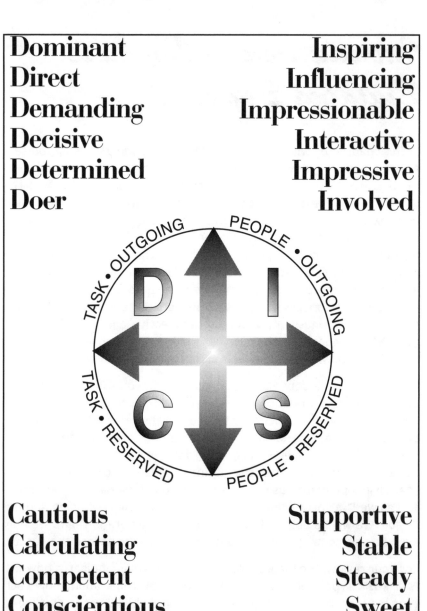

Cautious   **Supportive**
Calculating   **Stable**
Competent   **Steady**
Conscientious   **Sweet**
Contemplative   **Status quo**
Careful   **Shy**

"What should I wear when I show the Plan?" For women, a general suggestion is made about appropriate business attire. For men, a polite suggestion would be a business suit, white shirt, and a tie with some red in it. Now, how will the four personality types go about finding the "right" tie to wear when showing the Plan?

Danny Dunit, the **D** type Independent Business Owner, will take immediate action! He tackles this as he tackles life, meeting the challenge. He won't just go shopping for a new tie — Danny will hunt down a trophy-worthy tie, trap it, bag it, and bring it home! Conquering that tie is no problem! He probably won't bring along his wife as a hunting guide, although he may delegate this minor detail to her, if she can do it *today*. If she is too busy, Danny goes to the upscale mall department store where he occasionally "hunts" to "bag" his choice there. His hectic schedule leaves no time to visit several stores for the perfect tie; he just finds a *power tie* that conveys authority and status. Does the tie have red in it? Hopefully, it does; if it does not, Danny does not hesitate to bend the rules a bit, sure that his power tie is fine. He is back on the cell phone in his car within a few minutes. Danny Dunit puts on his tie and is off to show the Plan.

Irving Presley (Elvis' unknown twin) is our **I** type Independent Business Owner. Irving wants a splashy tie! His favorite magazine, *People*, hasn't shown many guys in ties lately, but as he buys the latest *People*, he talks to the clerk about pictures she could show him of businessmen in cool ties. She laughs and points him to *GQ*. After flipping through those pictures and talking to the people nearest him for their idea of the coolest tie, he heads off to the department store. On the way, he stops by the chocolate chip cookie stand... looks in the windows of the toy store... checks the shoe store for socks that might go with his tie... or maybe suspenders to match! Eventually he arrives at the department store just as the loudspeaker announces that there are only fifteen minutes left before closing. He feels so lucky when he proudly shows his wife his tie. The red splash on his tie is the noses of circus clowns! He is even happier when his wife quietly says, "No one will miss seeing you in that tie." Irving is sure that this business is going to be fun!

Sam Steady, an **S** type, is just not sure that he needs a new tie. Maybe he could use the same tie that he wore to his family reunion. He will take some time to think about the tie that he already has and will ask his wife and his upline if it would be a good one. He may browse through several stores to see if another tie might please them more. When his wife suggests a tie that she likes, he feels that she must want him to get a new tie. He spends a long time in the tie department without narrowing down the choices to one tie, so he brings home several ties, planning to return all but the one she likes the best. Even then, he still worries about his choice. If someone notices and compliments his tie, he wonders if it is too bold, even though the red is a small part of the foulard pattern. He really would have been more comfortable in his old tie, but he does like this one, and his wife is happy. Now that he has his tie, he begins to worry about standing in front of people to Show the Plan...

Carl Ruler, our **C** type Independent Business Owner, asks several questions so he can make the right tie choice. Clear guidelines will help him choose the best tie. Does his upline have a stated policy on dress? Should the tie be silk or synthetic-blend? Exactly how much red should be in the tie? Is there a preferred pattern for the tie? With his questions answered, he proceeds to the store. He takes his suit jacket with him to coordinate the colors. He puts a packaged dress shirt inside the coat and lays the tie against it — then walks around with it to view the interplay of colors under different lights. He settles on a tie with a classic pattern that is more tastefully burgundy than truly red. He is sure his upline intended for him to get burgundy, because red is just too loud for a business tie. Before making a final decision, he visits several stores to make sure he is getting the best price and the best choice. He is quietly pleased with the correctness of his choice, until he hears another Independent Business Owner mention buying a tie in the Personal Shopper® catalog... why was he not told about those ties earlier? Perhaps he can return his tie and get one from the catalog before he Shows the Plan...

Now you are probably thinking, "All that for a tie! I never dreamed there were such different ways to pick a tie!" What a difference personality makes in your approach to a business basic! Your approach may not be exactly like these men, but in reading about them, you can begin to see how your business approach is colored by your personality, too.

STYLE PREFERENCES AND PATTERNS

We have **DISC**overed that each type has a different natural perspective on something. Each **DISC** type applies their unique approach to every part of the business. The **D**s have confidence in conquering a task and tend to lack self-doubt. They will decisively insist, "*MY WAY* is the best way to do it!" **I**s find ways to make work fun and to involve people in anything they do. They love to shout, "This is the *FUN WAY* to do it." **S**s will rehearse the Plan in their minds until it feels friendly and comfortable, then work at a patient, steady pace until it is finished. They pat your arm and say, "Don't worry. We can do it together. This is the *EASY WAY*." **C**s plan their work, and then work their plan. They might say, "I can show you the *RIGHT WAY* to do it."

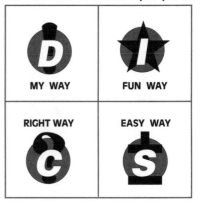

D MY WAY	**I** FUN WAY
C RIGHT WAY	**S** EASY WAY

Stewart shares how he began to understand this even as a boy:

> *My dad would often give my brother and me the same chore to finish by a certain time. When the time came, Dad would come back and I would have the chore finished, but my brother would still be planning the right way to do it. I may not have done it the easiest or best way, but I did manage to get it done. I soon began to realize that talking to my (High C) brother before I started would often make my (High D) work much easier. I could use his plan to speed up my work!*

Stewart recognized that different styles have different strengths as they approach their work. He learned to use his brother's strength in planning with his strength in doing. You will find this is true in the business as well. Your approach to the business may be effective in contacting, while your upline may suggest ways to adapt your approach to showing the Plan so that you may be more effective.

Goal setting is emphasized in our society today and can be very easy for us to do—it is accomplishing those goals that presents the challenge! An archery target is huge compared with the tiny bull's eye in the center. Anyone can see the bull's eye, but understanding and developing your skill empowers you to hit the bull's eye. We all can write down goals, but as we understand our preferred approach, we can develop the type of approach to those goals that empowers us to accomplish them too.

Ds are empowered by a challenging goal. They are energized by a goal they set that is very difficult! Let someone else do the easy part. It will

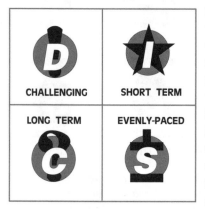

CHALLENGING   SHORT TERM

LONG TERM   EVENLY-PACED

not be worth their effort. **I**s live in the moment, so they need short-term goals with immediate rewards. The recognition they receive from a daily phone call may keep them working toward the goal better than a monthly meeting. Be patient with **S**s by remembering "slow and steady wins the race." They will start slowly, so do not start with unrealistic goals, but they are good finishers, because once they are comfortable, they will stick to a routine until they finish. They will also need your affirmation along the way. **C**s will carefully plan first, setting a realistic goal with long-term benefit. Their consistent, conscientious effort will continue to empower them to reach their goal. They may need your confidence that they are prepared to begin.

The following four chapters highlight the four **DISC** types of *Basic Business Building Styles*. As you read each chapter, you will identify with them more or less according to the high types in your style. All **DISC** types build the business, so see if you recognize anyone else in these pages!

A TAKE ACTION

CHAPTER FOUR

PERSONAL ACTION PLAN

In 25 words or less, describe your personality style as if you were talking to someone who wanted to better understand how to communicate with you.

_____

_____

_____

_____

_____

_____

_____

_____

_____

_____

High D Basic Building Styles

THE HIGH D TYPE AS AN INDEPENDENT BUSINESS OWNER

How does a high *D* approach the business? Like anything else, it is another world to conquer! There is a little bit of Alexander the Great in every high *D*. A high *D* is dominant; they will not be overlooked.

 The exclamation point represents the power of this style! They are demanding, first of themselves, and then also of others. We can admire their boldness and willingness to tackle difficult tasks. *D*s are direct, saying what they mean and meaning what they say. They echo the words of Napoleon, "Circumstances? I make circumstances!" *D*s are determined to make things happen! They bring this strength to the business, where they not only drive themselves, but can also motivate others to achieve.

*D*s are decisive and directive, so they may see themselves like the leader of a great army, commanding regiments of foot soldiers and equipment. However, this business is more like a volunteer army, where leadership comes to those who achieve by doing and serving others. A *D* type will need to learn that serving is part of the dream so that he or she can be a doer in serving too. They need to remember their Secret Tip!

SECRET TIP:
Before you can be IN authority you must first learn to be UNDER authority.

We say that **D**s are dogmatic, because they are so confident. They believe that if the dream is big enough, the facts don't count! They may not recognize that they need help missing the pitfalls that are sure to come as they deal with people, but they are diligent, hard workers. Their dynamic personality type can be the driving force behind a great organization!

D TYPES ARE...

GOAL-ORIENTED
PERFORMANCE CONSCIOUS
HARD TO PLEASE
SELF-CONFIDENT
INDUSTRIOUS
FIRM

As we learn how to Sponsor with Style, Dr. Rohm shares the main traits of **D** types in the business. This detailed description of each trait may be a good motivator for you or another high **D** Independent Business Owner.

GOAL-ORIENTED: **D**s will quickly and easily write down ambitious goals which most people would find nearly impossible. They want specific goals, clearly categorized by number of contacts per day, closing ratios, number of phone calls, time allocated per call, PV/BV level to achieve, etc. They will jump right in to reach for the dream and make it happen!

PERFORMANCE CONSCIOUS: Reaching the goal is very important for the **D**. They work hard! This is great in the business because they will make things happen and get results.

HARD TO PLEASE: Because they always strive for higher results, they are not easily satisfied with their own achievements. The high **D** upline must also learn to value the effort of their downline, or they may seem too hard to please and cause discouragement without realizing what they have done.

SELF-CONFIDENT: **D**s are naturally self-confident and will attempt the impossible—they can charge hell with a water gun! They will need to learn equal confidence in the System, so that they can use it to their benefit, instead of trying to improve upon it the first day! Learning to listen to others who are not as forceful or whose ideas differ theirs is a challenge for the high *D*. Their natural confidence will breed confidence in them and the business.

INDUSTRIOUS: *D*s don't just talk about it, they do it. They are task-oriented, not people-oriented, so they will make sure the work gets done. The high *D* will need to work with the people in their business, not in spite of those people.

FIRM: Once a *D* decides, almost nothing can change their direction. This firmness is great in the business if what they believe in is correct, but if it isn't they can cause problems. A high *D* must remember that other people may see important factors of which they were not aware, factors that may affect their direction. Their firmness can be a protective asset to an organization when difficult leadership is required.

Now do you have a feel for the strengths of the high *D* personality type? They are truly dynamic people in the business! Understanding what *D*s don't like will show us traits that can make the business a real struggle for them.

Let's review what high *D*s don't like and how it relates to the business:

> **_D_ TYPES DON'T LIKE...**
>
> INDECISION
> SLOW PEOPLE
> TALKERS WHO DON'T PRODUCE
> LAZY PEOPLE
> DETAILED ACTIVITIES
> TAKING ORDERS

INDECISION: This really drives a *D* crazy! A *D* wants to make the decision and move on. If someone else is responsible for the decision, the *D* will need to help them reach their decision by finding the cause for the indecision. A high *S* struggles with indecision and may simply need help deciding to decide. A high *C* can be indecisive if he or she thinks that more information is needed. The *D* may be able to supply more information, or show how the decision can be made with the available information.

SLOW PEOPLE: "Either lead, follow, or get out of the way!" *D*s really do feel this way! The high *S* will most often feel slow to them.

They may be married to a high **S** whose strengths they can learn to appreciate in other slow people. **D**s will need to learn not to "write off" people who may be the very ones they need to finish what they started.

TALKERS WHO DON'T PRODUCE: **D**s really dislike people who talk and talk and talk about building their business, but don't get out there and do it. People with a high **I** style may seem like empty talkers to them. If they can learn to appreciate fun with the high **I** style because it generates contacts, they may be able to help that talker produce too.

LAZY PEOPLE: In every organization there will be individuals who really just seem lazy and will not commit the time and effort to build a business. The **D** type will often sense a person's serious commitment to building the business and recognize potential achievers. The **D**s standard of commitment may be too high for people-oriented high **I**s and **S**s, so **D**s may need to distinguish between laziness and people-orientation.

DETAILED ACTIVITIES: Putting it mildly, the bottom line is almost everything to the high **D**! Detailed activities can seem like a barrier to completion for them, so they will often decide that they know enough facts and start work before they really should. Understanding that the high **C**s details can often help them achieve the goal more easily or quickly may motivate them to delegate these details and wait for their input. Remember this from the story at the beginning of this chapter about Stewart and his brother?

TAKING ORDERS: **D**s love to give orders but find taking orders more difficult. The structure of the business requires the high **D** to take orders and sometimes to pass on their upline's directions. The high **D** will want to improve those directions, but their upline may feel they are trying to take control. Learning from the high **S** taking orders and remembering their Secret Tip will help the high **D** stay under control and earn a place of leadership.

Under Control the high **D** is powerful in the business. That strength pushed to an extreme goes out of control and can do powerful damage in your business. Each personality style has strengths that can serve them well; but those same traits out of control can be very harmful.

Let us see how the Under Control/Out of Control high *D* relates to the business:

UNDER CONTROL/OUT OF CONTROL

COURAGEOUS .... RECKLESS
QUICK TO RESPOND .... RUDE
GOAL-ORIENTED .... IMPATIENT
RESULTS-ORIENTED .... PUSHY
DELIBERATE .... DICTATORIAL
SELF-CONFIDENT .... CONCEITED
DIRECT .... OFFENSIVE
SELF-RELIANT .... ARROGANT
STRAIGHTFORWARD .... ABRASIVE
COMPETITIVE .... RUTHLESS

COURAGEOUS: The *D* will gladly take on the business challenge of making the calls, driving the miles and meeting the obstacles, no matter what they might be. Pushed out of control, they can become RECKLESS by doing or saying things to accomplish their goals that may hurt the people involved.

QUICK TO RESPOND: Ask a *D* a question and they may answer you before you finish the question. They are quick to respond directly and to-the-point. Out of control, they may come across as RUDE. Because the high *D* is determined to get results, small talk seems pointless, and they will often miss the sensitivity to people it can afford. Others may find their quickness to respond overbearing and rude when they never mean to give that impression.

GOAL-ORIENTED: They not only set goals — they achieve them! In the business, once a *D* makes up their mind to do something, they drive for the goal. If the goal seems more difficult than they expected or than they deem worthy, they can become IMPATIENT. Leadership is a natural part of their style and business goals, so they may become impatient to assume leadership roles before they are offered or earned.

RESULTS-ORIENTED: The task orientation of a *D* will keep them very focused on getting the results they desire. And results are important! It is difficult to measure intent, desire, or excitement, but anyone can measure results! A high *D* needs to remember that others may not share this drive, and if they become PUSHY, they will not like the results. They must understand that "winning at any price" may cost them with people in ways they will later regret.

DELIBERATE: *D*s do things very deliberately and must have a purpose for doing anything. They enjoy strategy and planning every step they will take in building the business. They are sure that their plan will work. In their determination, they can quickly become DICTATORIAL, if they force people to fit into their plan. People may withdraw from working with them and the high *D* will not understand why.

SELF-CONFIDENT: The high *D* believes they can overcome any barrier or solve any problem. This confidence sustains them as they build the business. Too easy or quick a success may let the high *D* become CONCEITED and people will quietly walk away because they feel the high *D* cares only for themselves.

DIRECT: You will always know exactly where you stand with a *D*! They say what they mean, and mean what they say. They will ask for the order directly, saying, "Would you like to take the IBO opportunity and start your own business?" As they deal with people, they will be direct to address a problem instead of holding a grudge. When a difficult or complicated situation needs to be handled with sensitivity, their directness can feel OFFENSIVE and may alienate the people involved.

SELF-RELIANT: *D*s take care of themselves and will rely first on themselves to get the results they want. They encourage others by their example and in words to believe that they can also build the business. Out of control, they become ARROGANT, thinking that they can accomplish their dreams alone. They may forget that they need many different people to build an organization.

STRAIGHTFORWARD: What you see is what you get with a high *D*. They clearly tell you about the situation and what they want to accomplish. Because the goal is so important to them, they discount their own feelings in a situation and can easily become ABRASIVE to people when they just as easily discount the feelings of others. They expect people to choose to feel how they have chosen to feel. They need to learn to be considerate of others, realize that others feel differently, and respect those feelings. The high *D* will benefit from the better relationships that this respect will build for them.

COMPETITIVE: A *D* loves to make anything a game that they can win! They see competition as a natural motivation to do better. In this business, their competitive spirit will spur them on. If they become RUTHLESS in order to win, they will hurt many people, including themselves. They must learn the truth that all of us are better than just one of us!

The conversation of a high *D* tends to be bottomline and to the point. They make flat statements and challenge the comments of others. They really do not need the facts someone uses to support their comments — they want to know instead that the speaker really believes what he or she says and will stand behind those words with actions. They do not mean to offend others and are surprised if someone feels affronted by their straightforward approach. If you can understand that this is an issue of style, you can more easily accept and forgive whatever the high *D* does that goes against your style.

In the business, when you want something done quickly, give it to a high *D*!

Powerful IDEA

You can anticipate that they may have their first leads list made before you ask for it. They will be Showing the Plan before they are really ready. You will be more successful in teaching them by giving them acceptable choices for their business. They will naturally resist if they feel that they have diminished control or authority. This type will often choose to do something their way, then ask forgiveness rather than ask permission. They need to find someone in their upline whom they respect, to coach them and to whom they can be accountable. Having a coach in today's business world is important, if not critical to success.

We want to encourage you if you have a high **D** style, and also encourage those who have sponsored **D**s in the business. **D**s have some of these great strengths that will help them build their organizations:

Overcoming obstacles

Seeing the big picture

Getting started

Driving the group to progress

Accepting challenges without fear

Maintaining focus on goals

Getting results

Handling pressure

Being a self-starter

Delegating tasks

Projecting self-assurance

Providing leadership

Handling several tasks at the same time

CHAPTER FIVE
PERSONAL ACTION PLAN

Question 1: In the chart (page 78) "*D* Types Are..." if you have a high *D* style, explain the trait that is your greatest strength.

_____

Question 2: If you do not have a high *D* style, explain the trait that you most admire in someone with this style. _____

_____

Question 3: In the chart (page 79) "*D* Types Don't Like..." explain the trait that is hardest for you to deal with: _____

_____

Question 4: In the chart (page 81) "*D*s Under Control/Out of Control," explain the trait with which you struggle most, and why:

_____

_____

Question 5: Select two high *D* traits that could help you better build your organization: _____

_____

High I Basic Building Style

THE HIGH *I* TYPE
AS AN INDEPENDENT BUSINESS OWNER

How does an inspiring, influencing, impressive, imaginative *I* see their IBO business? The same way they see everything else: this is their most exciting experience!

What could we give the high *I* that would be better than a big red star? Maybe two?! This symbol recognizes their type with that red star! Life for this type is six fun Saturdays in a week! They always find ways to make work into play. We can admire this ability to brighten almost any situation. They live by the words of comic Joe E. Lewis: "You only live once — but if you work it right, once is enough!"

The high *I* experiences everything and loves to express what they feel in that experience! They are carefree and outgoing because they are naturally trusting, even to the point of sincere gullibility. The high *I* may exhibit more confidence than ability because they tend to be very optimistic and disinterested in details. They are engulfed by each experience, so they can easily make life an emotional roller coaster for everyone. They can feel higher than a kite one minute and lower than a skunk the next. They make friends easily because they certainly feel that a stranger is just a friend they have not met! More reserved types

SECRET TIP:
It's NICE to be important, but it's more IMPORTANT to be nice.

may feel overpowered by them and shy away from their open, emotional advance, but we all love the fun we have with them! Their fun comes right into the business with them!

Being without a definite plan is not a problem for a friendly, fun-loving, and impressionable *I* who is happy just talking with people. They will need help learning to listen because each thing they hear seems to remind them of something else they need to say! Their ability to meet and make new friends can boost their business, but they will always need to remember to take time in their fun to get down to some serious business.

Educational tapes let them feel like they know the business leaders through the stories that the leaders share. They experience these stories again as they tell the stories to others when they show the Plan, follow up, train, and coach. They may learn well from inspirational books when they can enter into the experience expressed. They enjoy the training sessions and functions because they love to interact with other people in the business!

I TYPES ARE...

FUN TO WATCH
GREAT STARTERS
POOR FINISHERS
LIKEABLE
PRONE TO EXAGGERATE
EASILY EXCITABLE

As we learn how to *Sponsor with Style*, Dr. Rohm shares the main traits of *I* types in the business. This detailed description of each trait may be a good motivator for you or another high *I* Independent Business Owner.

FUN TO WATCH: *I*s don't go to the party, they take the party with them! They will make any meeting fun and inspiring, which will attract people to the business. Home meetings will be as fun as major functions.

GREAT STARTERS: It is very easy for an *I* to start their business and write their prospect list. This excitement will carry them for awhile, but with time they will gradually lose interest and stop working the business to start working on another exciting project. Attending functions will give them fresh enthusiasm.

POOR FINISHERS: For high *I*s, starting a project is just much more fun than working through to finish it! They can miss some great results in the business because they just don't quite finish. Remembering to bring their conversations to their conclusion can be a struggle for them because they are easily distracted by something that looks like more fun.

LIKEABLE: Everyone likes a high *I*! They get us excited about our dreams and draw us into the business. We enjoy the high *I* because they enjoy us too!

PRONE TO EXAGGERATE: The last movie a high *I* saw was the *best* movie they have *ever* seen! The last restaurant they ate at was the *best* restaurant they have *ever* been to! They make us long to try it too! Can *every* movie be the *best*? This tendency to exaggerate can cause the *I* credibility problems in the business. Some people may really believe everything the *I* says and then be very disappointed when something does not turn out to be as grand as the *I* presented it would be. *D*s and *C*s may often smile and ignore what the high *I* says. Their business will suffer when their sensational stories become incredible.

EASILY EXCITABLE: The high *I* is easily excitable to the extreme. When they feel like business is too slow, it is terrible—they are losing *everything*! The high *I* who feels like this may, talk to everyone about how *bad* things are and discourage everyone around them. When business is good it is *wonderful* — the best it has ever been! Now they will attract many people to the business. Count on the high *I* to build excitement!

Now do you have a feel for the strengths of the high *I* personality type? They are truly exciting people in the business! Understanding what *I*s don't like will show us traits that can make the business a real struggle for them.

I TYPES DON'T LIKE...

BEING IGNORED
BEING ISOLATED
BEING RIDICULED
REPETITIVE TASKS
DETAIL WORK
LONG-TERM PROJECTS

Let's review what high *I*s don't like and how it relates to the business:

BEING IGNORED: You just have to notice the high *I*! They want to be liked and love to be the center of attention. If they feel ignored, they may grab the chance to talk even when you are in the middle of a conversation.

BEING ISOLATED: Put an *I* into a room by themselves and they find a way to get out of there! If they are in your organization, make sure to include them so they will never feel isolated. It is very important to keep an *I* plugged in to spread excitement.

BEING RIDICULED: What people think of them is very important, so they will take being ridiculed very personally. They want everyone in their organization to like them and can quickly be hurt if a *D* or *C* criticizes or laughs at them.

REPETITIVE TASKS: Doing something over and over again is soooo boring! They may talk someone else into doing it, but chances are good that they will find something more exciting to do.

DETAIL WORK: The details of the business will often frustrate high *I*s. They will try to rationalize that the detail isn't important and that having fun and getting people excited is more important. They may need to remember that money is a detail of the business that can make the other details important to them.

LONG-TERM PROJECTS: It is hard for an *I* to stay focused on a long-term project. The recognition from a long-term project will seem too far away to excite them. They need to have short-term goals for their business with immediate rewards that will help keep their interest. Involving many people in their projects will help them stay involved, too.

Under Control the high **I** is influential in the business. That strength pushed to an extreme goes out of control and can do incredible damage in your business. Each personality style has strengths that can serve them well; but those same traits out of control can be very harmful.

Let us see how the Under Control/Out of Control high **I** relates to the business:

UNDER CONTROL/OUT OF CONTROL

OPTIMISTIC	UNREALISTIC
PERSUASIVE	MANIPULATIVE
EXCITED	EMOTIONAL
COMMUNICATIVE	GOSSIPY
SPONTANEOUS	IMPULSIVE
OUTGOING	UNFOCUSED
FERVENT	EXCITABLE
INVOLVED	DIRECTIONLESS
IMAGINATIVE	DAYDREAMING
WARM/FRIENDLY	PURPOSELESS

OPTIMISTIC: They are cheerleaders for their group, always looking for someone to cheer on to victory in the business! They can really encourage the group through some difficult times. Pushed to an extreme, they can be UNREALISTIC as their optimism loses credibility when they overlook facts essential to potential results and benefits, or the complexity of a problem they must face.

PERSUASIVE: They are engaging talkers and enjoy telling stories about important people they may have met. It is simply amazing how many people they know! They also have a talent for weaving yarns, drawing from many examples they have heard from many sources into their discussions about the business. They can draw many people into the business in this way, but if their stories bend the facts too far, others will feel they are MANIPULATIVE, simply trying to get people to do what benefits the high **I**. This manipulation can cause huge resentment and seriously damage an organization.

EXCITED: They are so excited, and their excitement is infectious! Their organization will attract and energize people when a high **I** is on stage! They make work so much fun that achieving great goals seems possible, even worth trying to reach! If they face disapproval or public embarrassment because in their excitement they promise what they will not deliver, they can become EMOTIONAL and explode with an unexpected attack. They can become more consistent (and therefore more credible) in the business when they are accountable to someone to help them remember to do what they said they would do when they were excited enough to make a commitment.

COMMUNICATIVE: They do not hesitate to say almost anything to anyone! How easily the high *I* can start a conversation or explain their point of view! Showing the Plan is easy for them. Most people find it easy to listen to them and enjoy being around them. People are attracted to them for encouragement and coaching; because they like to talk and share what they know and whom they know, they can be GOSSIPY, sharing private information without meaning to hurt. This hurt may easily divide and damage people in an organization. A high *I* can learn to recognize privileged information to protect the privilege of knowing that person.

SPONTANEOUS: Life would be much less fun without the spontaneity of the high *I*. They are always ready to enter a door of opportunity that can lead to unexpected results in the business. Out of control, their spontaneous nature can become IMPULSIVE and burn up their energy without producing business results.

OUTGOING: The outgoing *I* will go to a party and know everyone there before they leave. This is great in prospecting for building the business! Trying to be involved in too many opportunities can make them UNFOCUSED; they may need to focus on the most promising opportunities to promote the business.

FERVENT: When they believe in the business they *really* believe! They will be so convinced that they are fervent about getting the word out and getting others involved. Sometimes they can seem so EXCITABLE that people won't believe the opportunity they describe is real or attainable. They may believe that every IBO will sponsor six new Directs their first month!

INVOLVED: The high *I* loves to be in the middle of whatever is happening! Because they so enjoy activity, they may be DIRECTIONLESS in their participation and miss opportunities to promote their business.

IMAGINATIVE: What ideas this *I* type can create! Their imagination can conceive what most of us would not dare to dream. Such dreams can be a wonderful motivator in this business. However, imagination can replace reality when DAYDREAMING takes over with ideas that have no purpose or use in achieving the dream.

WARM/FRIENDLY: Everyone feels that the high *I* is their friend because of the warm, friendly feeling they receive from the *I*. Because the business is built on relationships, their business will prosper. Unfortunately, the high *I* can be superficially friendly and become PURPOSELESS in getting the results for business success.

 Conversations with *I* types can be lengthy and free ranging, because one thing just leads to another! They tend to make emotional rather than rational statements and often will think out loud. They can jump quickly from one idea to another and leave others questioning their conclusions. They tend to talk things out rather than think things through. Other styles must recognize that when the high *I* makes a pronouncement, they are verbally testing ideas. Then other styles can give them room to alter their opinions. If you can understand that this is an issue of style, you can more easily accept and forgive whatever the high *I* does that goes against your style.

You may have heard business leaders say that their business really got going when it moved from their head to their heart. High *I* style Independent Business Owners usually start in their heart! They may struggle getting the business out of their heart and into their hands and eventually to their feet! Their talk and their feelings about the business may be genuine, but translating their feelings into appropriate action may be more difficult for them. Understanding the need to make their commitment match their inspiration is key to their success in the business. They need to find someone in their upline with whom they feel rapport, to coach them and to whom they can be accountable. Having a coach in today's business world is important, if not critical to success.

If you can understand that this is an issue of style, you can more easily accept and forgive whatever the high *I* does that goes against your style.

We want to encourage you if you have a high *I* style, and also encourage those who have sponsored *I*s in the business. *I*s are some of the happiest people in the world. If they can just learn to focus and stay on track, there is no end to their potential. Their motto for success is, "Inch-by-inch, everything is a cinch; but by the yard it is all hard!" *I*s have some of these great strengths that will help them build their organizations:

Speaking persuasively

Responding well to surprises or unplanned changes

Expressing ideas

Accepting new people

Creating enthusiasm and excitement

Working well with others

Having a sense of humor

Keeping a positive attitude

Finding the "upside" to downturns

Putting others at ease

Being sensitive to the feelings and emotions of others

Encouraging the discouraged

CHAPTER SIX

PERSONAL ACTION PLAN

Question 1: In the chart (page 89) "**I** Types Are..." if you have a high **I** style, explain the trait that is your greatest strength.

_____

Question 2: If you do not have a high **I** style, explain the trait that you most admire in someone with this style. —————————

_____

Question 3: In the chart (page 90) "**I** Types Don't Like..." explain the trait that is hardest for you to deal with: ————————

_____

Question 4: In the chart (page 91) "**I**s Under Control/Out of Control," explain the trait with which you struggle most, and why:

_____

_____

Question 5: Select two high **I** traits that could help you better build your organization: ————————————————

_____

High S Basic Building Style

THE HIGH S AS AN INDEPENDENT BUSINESS OWNER

How does a steady, stable, supportive, serving **S** see their IBO business? The same way they see everything else: It is a group of people they can support to have a great business to share.

 This symbol shows a plus and minus sign to represent the ability of the high **S** to do more or less what they need to do to give their support for continued harmony among people. The high **S** is people-oriented, but reserved. While an **I** tends to be a "Here I am!" kind of person, an **S** is a "Here we are!" type. They love their home and family, and seek a steady and stable environment for everyone to share.

They primarily view their business as a group of people enjoying close relationships and sharing wonderful times together. It was probably a successful **S** who first said, "Even if there were no money to be made in this business, I would still be in it for the friends." A successful **D** probably responded, "Even if there weren't any friends, I'd still be in it for the money!" We must all remember that both are needed for success in this business!

Natural timidity can be a struggle for the high **S** because they do not want others to feel that they are pushy. The high **S** may need to remember how much they appreciated the person who showed them the business, so that they will feel comfortable sharing the Plan with others. You may have heard successful business couples say that one spouse "gets people in the business" and the other spouse "keeps them in." Often they mean that the outgoing one is good at stirring up enthusiasm in new Independent Business Owners, while the other is good at long-term relationship issues and can smooth over offenses and disappointments along the way. The latter is the strength of the high **S** in the business. It is easy for some to overlook or undervalue these gentle skills, but someone with a warm, quiet demeanor becomes a trusted friend everywhere. When someone is a friend of the high **S**, they may naturally expect too much help from them. The high **S** can keep their relationships more balanced when they recite their Secret Tip:

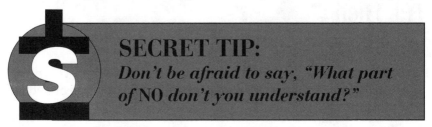

SECRET TIP:
Don't be afraid to say, "What part of NO don't you understand?"

Relationships really can keep people in the business at times when their dream is dead and their vision is hazy. Often the high **S** can give more or less what it takes to keep them in the business. There are high **S** Independent Business Owners who seldom show the Plan, but faithfully attend all of their upline's events because they enjoy the good feeling of getting together with positive people. Strong pressure to produce results might push them away. But when they are welcomed and encouraged to grow at their own pace, they can accomplish too. They may achieve for affirmation from their upline, rather than for the money earned. For these slower-paced people, this axiom is essential: Give yourself time to succeed. There are many highly successful Independent Business Owners who have a high **S** personality style, proving that "if you can build a relationship, you can build a business."

S TYPES ARE...

SWEETEST PEOPLE IN THE
WORLD
EASILY MANIPULATED
LOYAL FRIENDS
TEAM PLAYERS
POOR STARTERS

As we learn how to *Sponsor with Style*, Dr. Rohm shares the main traits of high **S** types in the business. This detailed description of each trait may be a good motivator for you or another high **S** Independent Business Owner.

SWEETEST PEOPLE IN THE WORLD: Looking into the eyes of a high *S* will show you what sweet really means. The high *S* needs the affirmation of others and seeks it by being supportive. In their business they will support and care for each of their Independent Business Owners. Each one in their organization will feel that they are such nice people.

EASILY MANIPULATED: One of the biggest struggles for the high *S* in the business, as in life, is that they are easily manipulated. They can be persuaded to do things to keep harmony when they really do not want to do them. Harmful results to their business or other people may upset them more than the disharmony of refusal in the beginning.

LOYAL FRIENDS: If you ever wanted a good friend, you will find one in a high *S*. They will be very loyal to people in the business and to using the products.

TEAM PLAYERS: They will see the business as a huge team of people where they are so happy to be included. As they sponsor individuals they will gently draw them into the team and the benefits of being included.

POOR STARTERS: The high *S* will hesitate to start anything new, especially in business, until they feel comfortable that good results are predictable. They will be concerned about being rejected or offending a friend.

GREAT FINISHERS: Even though they are poor starters, they are great finishers. It makes them feel uneasy when there are many unfulfilled promises. They value their routine, and when they commit to the business, they will continue when others give up.

Now do you have a feel for the strengths of the high *S* personality type? They are truly steady people in the business! Understanding what *S*s don't like will show us traits that can make the business a real struggle for them.

S TYPES DON'T LIKE...

INSENSITIVITY
TO BE YELLED AT
MISUNDERSTANDINGS
SARCASM
SURPRISES
BEING PUSHED

Let's review each area and how it relates to the business:

INSENSITIVITY: Other more task-oriented styles may not realize that their actions have hurt other people. This can offend the high **S**, who will always be sensitive to how IBOs, prospects, and families are being treated. Because they hate confrontation, the high **S** may never say anything to the offender, but may try to comfort the other person. As a group grows they will contribute a kindness that will keep people in the business.

TO BE YELLED AT: Others may be frustrated by the slow, steady pace of the high **S**. In their frustration, other types may try to push the high **S** by yelling at them. Conflict and disagreements cause the **S** to shut down and will never motivate them. When others in the business may be quick to conflict, the high **S** can help others find harmony with their support and calm attitude.

MISUNDERSTANDINGS: They hate misunderstandings because they need everyone in the business to understand each other and work in harmony. They will continue efforts to maintain harmony through understanding.

SARCASM: Since they want everyone to like each other, they will not want sarcasm to hurt their friends, who are all the members of their organization.

SURPRISES: Don't think that surprises will excite the high **S**. They will not accept changes quickly or without some pain of adjustment. Changes in the corporate approach, or showing the Plan differently will cause stress in their lives until they feel that the new way is friendly and can be trusted.

BEING PUSHED: Because they are easily manipulated, you may think that the high *S* could be easily pushed around. They may be manipulated easily to keep harmony or help someone, but if you try to change their routine quickly they can become very quietly stubborn and resist your speed or any change at all.

Under Control the high *S* is steady in the business. That strength pushed to an extreme goes Out of Control and can do foundational damage in your business. Each personality style has strengths that can serve them well; but those same traits out of control can be very harmful.

Let us see how the Under Control/Out of Control high *S* relates to the business:

UNDER CONTROL/OUT OF CONTROL

RELAXED	LACKING INITIATIVE
RELIABLE	DEPENDENT .
COOPERATIVE	A "SUCKER"
STABLE	INDECISIVE
GOOD LISTENER	UNCOMMUNICATIVE
SINGLE-MINDED	INFLEXIBLE
STEADFAST	RESISTANT TO CHANGE
SOFTHEARTED	EASILY MANIPULATED
SYSTEMATIC	SLOW
AMIABLE	RESENTFUL

RELAXED: Their relaxed and easygoing style will bring stability and comfort to the organization. In their hesitation, they can be **LACKING INITIATIVE** and let many opportunities pass by.

RELIABLE: At every function and meeting, they are reliable to be there for you. They will always do what they say they will do for you. Because they need your affirmation, they may become **DEPENDENT** on you and others and slow the group down.

COOPERATIVE: When the high *S* cares for you, they are very cooperative to help anywhere you need their help. To help you, they may sacrifice their own needs and can be **A "SUCKER"** and let others take advantage of their good nature.

STABLE: The high **S** brings stability to the organization because they appreciate the success of a proven routine. They are comfortable with things that stay the same in the business and will remind the other styles to think again before making a change. They can be INDECISIVE about choosing change even when it will make the business grow.

GOOD LISTENER: Each one in their group will appreciate what a great listener the high **S** is. They will give many hours supporting and caring for others. Even though they do so much listening they can be UNCOMMUNICATIVE about how they feel, thinking that their situations are not as bad as others so there is no need to talk about themselves. They can be left carrying their own burdens and the burdens of the rest of the world.

SINGLE-MINDED: Once a business system or method has been accepted by the group, they will be very true and faithful to the system; other ideas or methods may be presented but they will reject them. They can be INFLEXIBLE about trying new concepts that could really benefit them.

STEADFAST: You may be ready to skip to the next chapter of this book, but the steadfast **S** is comfortable at this point and will find insights that you may miss! They will be firm in using tried and proven methods in the business; even though times may change, they may be RESISTANT TO CHANGE that must occur for further business growth.

SOFTHEARTED: In a cold-hearted world, the high **S** will bring a tenderness and care that will really help others in the business. Unfortunately, through this kindness they can be EASILY MANIPULATED to serve the selfish intentions of others.

SYSTEMATIC: The high **S** will do paper work and show the Plan the same way over and over again. While being systematic ensures that they will get predictable results, others can be frustrated when the **S** is so concerned about following the system that they are too SLOW in getting things done.

AMIABLE: The high **S** is so friendly and kind, that amiable really describes them! If someone in the organization needs their help they will happily help them. Even if they continue to help, they may feel they are being taken advantage of and may inwardly become RESENTFUL and gradually withdraw their support of the business. Raising their **PQ** to do what is best for them too will help them prevent this resentment.

 Ss conversations tend to be filled with requests for affirmation such as, "How do you want me to do this? Am I doing it right?" What they need to hear from their Sponsor is, "You're doing fine, and I appreciate your concern...!" In their reluctance to be seen as pushy or assertive, they often keep their opinions and feelings to themselves unless they are asked or really feel hurt and angry. Do not assume that if they have an issue with you, they will confront it. Generally, they "stuff" their feelings because they want to avoid conflict. When you directly ask them about their feelings, they often diminish the intensity of their response because they can feel intimidated easily. Rather than confronting you or addressing their feelings, they may quietly continue doing things their own way. If you can understand that this is an issue of style, you can more easily accept and forgive whatever the high **S** does that goes against your style.

They need to find a friend in their upline who can help them learn to care for themselves the same way that they are so quick to care for others. Having this kind of friend as a coach in today's business world is important, if not critical to their success.

Everyone needs a friend in the business, and the high **S** is no exception. Even though the **S** has many friends, they need a special friend who will help them confront the difficult issues that they need to confront.

We want to encourage you if you have a high **S** style, and also encourage those who have sponsored **S**s in the business. **S**s have some of these great strengths that will help them build their organizations:

Showing sincerity

Including others

Being even-tempered

Emphasizing and demonstrating loyalty

Building stable relationships

Using an easier way to do things

Providing dependability

Finishing jobs that may have been started by others

Being a team player

Helping others in difficult times

Sharing hospitality

Offering others affirmation

CHAPTER SEVEN

PERSONAL ACTION PLAN

Question 1: In the chart (page 98) "**S** Types Are..." if you have a high **S** style, explain the trait that is your greatest strength.

_____

Question 2: If you do not have a high **S** style, explain the trait that you most admire in someone with this style. _____

_____

Question 3: In the chart (page 100) "**S** Types Don't Like..." explain the trait that is hardest for you to deal with: _____

_____

Question 4: In the chart (page 101) "**S**s Under Control/Out of Control," explain the trait with which you struggle most, and why:

_____

_____

Question 5: Select two high **S** traits that could help you better build your organization:_____

_____

High C Basic Building Style

THE HIGH C
AS AN INDEPENDENT BUSINESS OWNER

Last, but not least, how does a cautious, conscientious, calculating, correct **C** approach their business? The same way they see everything else: It is a Plan to implement to build a long-term, profitable business.

 This symbol shows a question mark to represent how the high **C** asks many questions. They love to bring order out of chaos by understanding a system and knowing how to make everything fit within it. They prize consistent quality and excellence. This preference carries over into their business, where they find it easier to complete correct order forms than to deal with Independent Business Owners.

If you have a question about a product, ask a high **C**! They carefully study all the product details and other issues that affect the business. Their conscientious attention to the facts builds quality and excellence in any organization. They like to document everything they do, to know the in-depth reason behind the in-depth reason. **C** types can be so precise that their handwritten paperwork sometimes looks as if it had been typed. Their concentrated effort to be completely correct may immobilize them from taking action on an issue like showing the Plan. They do not like carelessness in others and do not tolerate mistakes in themselves. They may need upline coaching for the confidence to allow themselves to risk imperfection when presenting the Plan. This lack of confidence can make others feel that they are cool or aloof. Making an effort to convey warmth will help the high **C** be more successful in the business. They too can remember their Secret Tip:

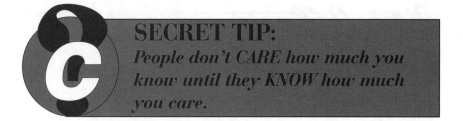

SECRET TIP:
People don't CARE how much you know until they KNOW how much you care.

They like to ask questions and verify answers. At times, others may feel their questions sound like, "What about this? What about that? What about the other thing? What about...?" *Always* another question? The high **C** does not understand how this could be a problem, since they still need to validate quality, detailed answers. They tend to analyze almost everything, and enjoy finding and correcting mistakes. People may feel that **C**s are picky or fault-finding, but they are simply convinced that anything worth doing is worth doing well. When they do reach a conclusion, they tend to draft firm and defined plans, and they will resist making unnecessary changes without solid reasoning. They will work the System to achieve business success.

C TYPES ARE...
PERFECTIONISTS
DIFFICULT TO SATISFY
LOGICAL
METICULOUS
SELF-SACRIFICING
INQUISTIVE

As we learn how to *Sponsor with Style*, Dr. Rohm shares the main traits of **C** types in the business. This detailed description of each trait may be a good motivator for you or another high **C** Independent Business Owner.

PERFECTIONISTS: In their business they will want everything done correctly. All the paperwork will be completed on time, checked and then rechecked.

DIFFICULT TO SATISFY: Because they are perfectionists, it will be difficult for anyone or anything in the business to completely satisfy them. They may always think of ways that something could have been done better. Because of their expectations, we may produce something better than we thought possible.

LOGICAL: They will carefully study every area of the business and think it through in a very logical manner. They will set up realistic goals in a logical order for their long-term achievement in the business.

METICULOUS: They may not have the largest business, but everything will be compartmentalized and carefully written out.

SELF-SACRIFICING: As they focus on correctly completing tasks of the business, they will often be self-sacrificing. In the business, they may sacrifice themselves so that something is really done correctly.

INQUISTIVE: They are naturally inquisitive because they desire to put things and ideas in boxes so that they can understand how things and concepts fit together and fit in the logical order of things. They will study every aspect of the business to find its order and understand how it ideally works.

Now do you have a feel for the strengths of the high *C* personality type? They are truly conscientious people in the business! Understanding what *C*s don't like will show us traits that can make the business a real struggle for them.

Let's review each area and how it relates to the business:

_C_ TYPES DON'T LIKE...

BEING CRITICIZED
MISTAKES
SUDDEN CHANGES
SHODDY WORK
UNPREPAREDNESS
UNNECESSARY INTERRUPTIONS

BEING CRITICIZED: They are their toughest critic, constantly requiring perfection in anything they do in the business. They find it difficult to deal with being criticized by others because they feel like a failure in missing the error and a double failure in creating the error originally. They expect perfection in an imperfect world.

MISTAKES: Often *C*s will choose to do a task alone simply because they don't like mistakes. Even though they are self-sacrificing, this extra burden may slow progress for the whole organization.

SUDDEN CHANGES: Since so much thought and time has been put into developing the system, then it makes no sense to change procedures suddenly. If we logically prove why a change is good, then we can cautiously do it correctly to ensure success. They usually will not recognize a need for any sudden changes.

SHODDY WORK: If you want a strong business, then build it the right way. A high *C* does not tolerate shoddy work, or understand why something might be done just "good enough." They expect you to live up to their own high standards.

UNPREPAREDNESS: The high *C* knows that we are sure to face unnecessary difficulty caused by unpreparedness. When we know all the facts, figures and answers about the business, we can keep this difficulty confined to unforeseen developments.

UNNECESSARY INTERRUPTIONS: Because the high *C* focuses intently on the task at hand, they detest unnecessary interruptions in their procedure or plans. Others may feel that their reaction to interruptions that inevitably come is simply cold or uncaring.

Under Control the high *C* is conscientious in the business. That strength pushed to an extreme goes Out of Control and can do intense damage in your business. Each personality style has strengths that can serve them well; but those same traits out of control can be very harmful.

Let us see how the Under Control/Out of Control high *C* relates to the business:

UNDER CONTROL/OUT OF CONTROL	
ORDERLY	COMPLUSIVE
LOGICAL	CRITICAL
INTENSE	UNSOCIABLE
CURIOUS	NOSEY
TEACHABLE	EASILY OFFENDED
CAUTIOUS	FEARFUL
CORRECT	RIGID
QUESTIONING	DOUBTFUL
CONSCIENTIOUS	WORRISOME
PRECISE	PICKY

ORDERLY: Their business will be very organized and structured, which will keep their system running smoothly. As their intense focus increases, they can become so concerned about every detail that they become COMPULSIVE about little issues that are not important. This frustrates people who work with them and may cause people to give up trying to satisfy the expectations of the high **C**.

LOGICAL: The high **C** must make logical sense of everything. They tend to ignore their feelings in favor of logical facts. They will carefully and completely think through every area of the business. In their unending quest for perfection, others may feel that they are just CRITICAL of everything and everybody. Out of control, their critical nature may drive people away from them and out of the business.

INTENSE: When they are focused on the business, nothing can pull them away. The world can totally pass them by, while they are reading all the detailed information about the business. As their intensity magnifies, they can become UNSOCIABLE, concentrating on details that seem more important to them than people are.

CURIOUS: The high **C** is insatiably curious. They just want the facts—all the facts! They have just one more question that needs to be answered before any conclusion can be drawn. This desire for the facts tends to make them NOSEY about others' personal lives. The high **C** may ignore their own feelings, but if they want to enjoy people in the business, they must learn to respect the feelings of others.

TEACHABLE: Their quest for knowledge and quality answers keeps the high **C** very teachable. They always want to learn new procedures in the business and understand what others are doing. When the suggestions take issue with the correctness of the way they are already conducting their business, they can be EASILY OFFENDED and defensive against all suggestions. They need to be convinced that their old way was right, but the new way is better.

CAUTIOUS: They are cautious, never wanting to make a mistake in their business. Their cautious nature can predict and prevent many costly mistakes in the business. They are constantly checking themselves, and may become so FEARFUL of breaking the rules,or not getting it right, that they can become immobilized.

CORRECT: The high **C** could say, "Do it right or don't do it at all!" They want to be correct, so they will follow the business Plan step by step. This intense need to follow the Plan in any area of the business can cause them to be too RIGID, not allowing for other possibilities to achieve their goals.

QUESTIONING: The high **C** is questioning. They ask the questions that must be asked and others have missed. If an answer depends heavily upon emotion, or really has no definite answer, they may become DOUBTFUL of everything and everybody and lose their focus in the business.

CONSCIENTIOUS: They will carefully cover every detail of their business. Every piece of paperwork will be completed, copied and filed on time. As their business expands, they will have a tendency to be WORRISOME over all the details that must be handled correctly.

PRECISE: All the numbers and facts given to you by a high **C** will most likely be correct. You can be sure that they are right about the business. Since they want to be so precise, they can easily become PICKY about others and the way they achieve their goals. They may need to show others why they feel the need to be so precise, or they can be perceived as a critic.

Channing Pollock once said, "A critic is a legless man who teaches running." It is possible for **C**s to be seen as this kind of a critic. However, with a small adjustment to their approach, another **C** word that could suit them as well would be "a coach." Because they are able to view circumstances less emotionally, they often can provide a more objective solution to a difficult situation. Others may also feel offended, thinking that the high **C** feels that no feelings have much merit, only their cool logic. If you can understand that this is an issue of style, you can more easily accept and forgive whatever the high **C** does that goes against your style.

Getting in touch with their own feelings is unnatural for the high **C**! They can raise their **PQ** by learning to value their feelings and the feelings of others in order to build a successful business. Their upline can coach them to understand how to do this. Having a sensitive coach in today's business world is important, if not critical to success, for the high **C**.

We want to encourage you if you have a high **C** style, and also encourage those who have sponsored **C**s in the business. **C**s have some of these great strengths that will help them build their organizations:

Working the Plan carefully

Being conscientious in their approach

Maintaining their focus on their plan

Objectively evaluating situations

Improving methods

Analyzing obstacles

Striving for logical outcomes

Organizing materials

Developing long-term objectives

Double-checking details

Providing accuracy

Assuring quality and accountability

A TAKE ACTION

CHAPTER EIGHT

PERSONAL ACTION PLAN

Question 1: In the chart (page108) "**C** Types Are..." if you have a high **C** style, explain the trait that is your greatest strength.

_____

Question 2: If you do not have a high **C** style, explain the trait that you most admire in someone with this style. _____

_____

Question 3: In the chart (page 109) "**C** Types Don't Like..." explain the trait that is hardest for you to deal with: _____

_____

Question 4: In the chart (page 111) **C**s "Under Control/Out of Control," explain the trait with which you struggle most, and why:

_____

_____

Question 5: Select two high **C** traits that could help you better build your organization: _____

_____

Celebrating Our Basic Building Styles

The previous four chapters have been an overview of predictable human behavior patterns as adapted in the business. It shows how each of the **DISC** types offers strengths, yet struggles with some difficulties as they relate to the business. Our personal observations and insights from a number of Diamonds have helped us to bring this chapter from theory to experience.

As you begin to recognize in your experience some of these traits from each of the **DISC** types, we hope that you will understand yourself in the business more fully.

As you use this chapter to raise your **PQ**, you can take the Second Step and begin to understand others.

The high **D** will see this as a way to more quickly accomplish their business goals.

The high **I** will want to talk to others in the business about the exciting information he or she is learning.

The high **S** will find that they can help their friends in the business more effectively by understanding their perspectives and feelings more completely.

The high **C** will work more effectively with people in the business because they will logically develop realistic expectations of others. Everyone is empowered to improve!

The chart on the next page, *Personality Perspectives*, can be a ready reference to your **DISC** Basic Building Styles.

Personality Perspectives	D	I	S	C
Outlook or Orientation:	Likes to lead or be in charge	Likes to persuade others	Likes to support and help	Likes consistent quality and excellence
Blind Spot:	Feelings of others	Recalling past commitments	Moving quickly on problems or issues	Seeing the big picture; Feelings
Response Under Pressure:	Abrasive Tough	Careless Unpredictable	Hesitant Indecisive	Picky Pessimistic
Secret Fear:	Being taken advantage of	Loss of social recognition	Change; Confrontation	The unknown; undefined
When they feel cornered:	Frontal attack	Emotional attack	Stubborn defense	Technical defense
Likes to do things:	The fastest way	The fun way	The traditional way	The proper way
Approach to tasks:	Do it now	Make it fun	Work together	Do it right
Approach to people:	Let's see what you can do	Let's have fun	Let's do something together	Let's do our own part

Let's have some fun to celebrate our progress! Do you have a pen or pencil handy? If not, please stop here and get one now. Reading about this is just not the same as doing it, so please go get that pen and...

On the first line below, sign your name as you would your normal signature.

_____

Nothing exceptional has happened so far, has it? Now, place the pen in your other hand, and write your name again, on the next line below. Really — do this! You will see why in a minute...

_____

When you used your less dominant hand, how did it feel? Did it feel awkward? Does your name look like you should have used a crayon instead of a pen? We do not often practice writing with our other hand! Did it require a little extra effort and concentration? Was it even a bit stressful as some of the letters tried to come out backwards? Who do you know who writes using the hand that seemed to give you so much trouble? Using this hand seems natural, usual, and normal to them! Do you think, with practice, that you could learn to write well with your other hand too? It may never feel as natural as your preferred hand, but you could learn, couldn't you?

TAKE ACTION

Now try this! Lay the book down in front of you right now, and clasp or fold your hands together in front of you. Interlace your fingers.

(Go ahead — don't feel silly because nobody is watching you!) Keeping your hands folded together, look at your thumbs. Does your right thumb rest on top of your left thumb, or do you do it the other way? If someone had asked you which way you fold your hands, would you have been able to tell them? Or would you have first had to clasp your hands together and then look down to see?

Now, completely pull your hands apart. Put them back together, but switch the position of your hands, not just moving one thumb over the other, but also the way your fingers interlace. (If your left forefinger was on top before, now the right forefinger should be on top, etc.) Did your fingers get tangled in the move? Sometimes this happens! Some people have the sensation that a finger is missing, while others feel as if they have added one. What would happen if you had to go through life folding your hands the *wrong* way? Would you ever stop feeling uncomfortable? Would you just stop folding your hands at all? Remember this feeling...

TAKE ACTION

Finally, cross your arms by folding them across your chest...

(Come on — you've been a good sport so far, and this is the last time!) Look down at your arms. Does your left arm cross over your right arm, or does your right cross over your left?

Who actually taught you to do it this way? How do you know it's the correct way to do it? Have you ever tried to do it the other way? Do you cross your arms the way you do, just to upset all the good people who do it the other way? You probably do it this way because it's the way you have always done it, and it's the way that feels the most natural to you! Do you see any need to change what is naturally comfortable for you?

> Just as there is no right way to cross your arms or fold your hands, there is not one personality style that is right for everyone! Our signatures are just as unique as we are.

Just as you felt uncomfortable folding your hands the *wrong* way, you may feel uncomfortable trying to see something from the personality perspective of another person who has a different style than yours. Do you see the relationship between these three exercises and the way we tend to look at people whose patterns are different from our own? Do you suppose they do the things they do to annoy us, or simply because they've done them this way, naturally, their whole lives? Dr. Rohm loves to remind us of this when he says, "People do not do things against you; they do things for themselves!"

In putting these personality insights to work for you, be careful to remember this: a strength for you may be a struggle for someone else, and their strength may cause you great struggles! Julie says that she can learn *something* from anyone. She loves to learn how another style can teach her the secrets of *their* success! Adapting her style using their secrets is Step Three in raising her **PQ**, *Adapting Your Style to Have Better Relationships.*

> We need better relationships because we are in a people business. We can learn from each other and grow together in the business as we keep the following attitude:

I seek your forgiveness for all the times I talked

when I should have listened;

Got angry when I should have been patient;

Acted when I should have waited;

Feared when I should have been delighted;

Scolded when I should have encouraged;

Criticized when I should have complimented;

Said no when I should have said yes;

And said yes when I should have said no.

– Marian Wright Edelman

WE RE ON OUR WAY TOGETHER
WHAT A GREAT WAY TO GO!

A TAKE
ACTION

CHAPTER NINE

PERSONAL ACTION PLAN

After having read chapters four through nine, you should have a better understanding of your personality style. In your own words, describe what you like best about your unique personality style. Also include what you need to be most aware of and need to keep under control.

_____

_____

_____

_____

_____

_____

_____

_____

_____

CHAPTER TEN

Styles at a Glance

If every prospect wore a Personality Insights pin with a **D**, **I**, **S**, or **C** on it, you would know how to approach each of them according to their personality style. You could make such a great first impression! In a way, people do wear their **DISC** pins in plain view... if you know what to look for.

Using the techniques in this chapter, you can learn to identify the highest type in your prospect's style. As you raise your **PQ**, this enables you to understand how your style naturally affects them and how to adapt your style to put them at ease. You are ready for a great relationship!

Psychologist Alfred Adler said, "I don't put people in boxes; I just keep finding them there." Putting anyone in a personality box is pointless, because each personality style has some traits from each type. But **DISC**overing their predominant type can really help us begin to mind our **P**s and **Q**s:

> **P**rize their personality perspective.

> **Q**uietly satisfy their style needs.

> **P**repare your thoughts and feelings to relate to them.

> **Q**uickly communicate encouragement to accomplish their dreams.

Three easy techniques will help you identify another person's style. As you become more acquainted with **DISC** you will find yourself often using the technique you prefer. You may be surprised by how much easier it is to quickly communicate and benefit from their perspectives on issues. You may have fun seeing someone's eyes brighten because you communicated encouragement for their dreams. You may feel their affirmation as you quietly satisfy their style needs. You may for the first time be able to truly prize a personality perspective that is foreign to yours. You may even find yourself being less critical of others and prizing the differences of each style.

The *Pointing* Technique

We call the first method to identify a person's style the Pointing Technique since you use your finger to guide you in finding someone's style. Do not start pointing at people. They may think you strange, and that is not how this works! Look at the circle below as you answer this question:

Question 1. Does this person usually seem fast-paced and outgoing, or is this person slower-paced and reserved? Point to that half of the circle.

Fast-paced, outgoing people are naturally inclined to speak and move with more energy, gestures, and facial expressions. They may "talk with their hands" as you converse. They may often be late to meetings or come into the room at the last minute. Slower-paced, reserved people are naturally inclined to speak and move more quietly, with more guarded gestures or gentle facial expressions. They may not show any physical reaction as you converse. They will often be a little early to meetings and enter the room slowly and carefully.

Now look at the next circle below as you answer this question:

Question 2. Does this person appear to be more task-oriented or more people-oriented? Point to that half of the circle.

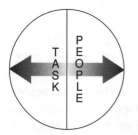

Task-oriented people tend to focus more on getting the job done or accomplishing the goal. They seem less influenced by the opinions of others, being *loners* instead of *joiners*. They will often talk about all the things they need to get done or how busy they are. As Independent Business Owners, they will talk more about products and the Plan than they talk about people. People-oriented individuals tend to enjoy the company of others more than doing projects. They are more influenced by the opinions of others, *more joiners than loners*. As Independent Business Owners, they will often talk about prominent people they know or fondly tell you about people in their downline or upline.

Now Point to the center of the **DISC** model of Human Behavior below. Putting together your two choices from the circles above, you can point to one quadrant in the **DISC** model of Human Behavior below:

If you chose Outgoing and Task-oriented, your finger will move up and to the left into the **D** quadrant.

If you chose Outgoing and People-oriented, your finger will move up and to the right into the **I** quadrant.

If you chose Reserved and People-oriented, your finger will move down and to the right into the **S** quadrant.

If you chose Reserved and Task-oriented, your finger will move down and to the left into the **C** quadrant.

Your finger should now be pointing to one of four quadrants of the circle displaying a **D**, an **I**, an **S**, or a **C**. See how easy it is to identify the predominant type in someone's style?

Now you can prepare your approach as you speak with your prospect, remembering that, according to "The Model of Human Behavior" diagram:

Ds are outgoing and task-oriented

Is are outgoing and people-oriented

Ss are reserved and people-oriented

Cs are reserved and task-oriented

The **Simply Ask** Technique

We say that to use the second technique, you must *Simply Ask*. Simply ask the person these two questions to help you identify the highest type in their personality style. Using this technique in countless presentations, product sales, prospecting, and just social situations, no one seems offended to answer two simple questions. We may have felt a little funny asking them, but no one seemed to mind answering them. Often, people will quickly answer the questions, then reply, "Why did you ask that?" This becomes an open invitation to engage in a meaningful conversation. Most people really appreciate an effort to better communicate with them. Open your doors of communication using this *Simply Ask* technique:

Simple ask these questions:

> Question 1.   Do you feel that you are more outgoing, or would you say you tend to be a little more reserved?

If a person responds by saying that they have some of both, you can reply, " That's true ! we all have some of both of these qualities. But if you had to choose between the two, in which direction would you lean?"

> Question 2.   Do you think you are more task-oriented or do you feel more people-oriented?

Again, remind them that we may have both qualities, but you are asking which way they most often lean. Remember, you don't have to ask these questions one after the other like a machine gun, but gently ask them in the flow of normal conversation. Most people really enjoy talking about themselves and seem genuinely pleased when you show interest in them. If you are asked why, explain that you are interested in understanding them better, and that this helps you to begin to understand them better.

THE *FORM* TECHNIQUE

We can remember the third technique for understanding a person's style from the acronym FORM. Using this FORM technique may take a little more time; we like to think of this as our advanced method since you must ask open-ended questions. Their answers may indicate the predominant type in their style. The FORM is:

F: FAMILY

Listen to their response about their spouse or children to **DISC**over if their description indicates that they are outgoing. Their conversation may reveal that they are more reserved instead. Also listen for an indication that they are more task-oriented or people-oriented.

For example:

"What do you enjoy most about your family?" — If they talk more about the characteristics of individuals they appreciate, they are probably more people-oriented. If they describe the roles and accomplishments of the individuals, they are probably more task-oriented.

Answer 1. "My husband is a dedicated doctor who really cares about his patients." This answer from the wife shows that she values who her husband is and that he cares for people. She is probably more people-oriented.

Answer 2. "My husband is a specialist who has a demanding practice." This answer would indicate that the wife values the work that her husband does and his expertise. She is probably more task-orientated.

Answer 3. "We love to go to different places and do new things together. We also enjoy great parties at home with many friends!" This answer would indicate that this person is probably outgoing.

Answer 4. "Our home is so peaceful and quiet. We enjoy reading wonderful books or working in our garden. We don't care for big groups or travel, except to visit family." This would probably indicate that they are more reserved.

Your skill will increase with practice as you understand that sometimes how the person describes what they enjoy is more important than what they actually say they enjoy. In a family, you are dealing with the personality styles of two or more people, so listen carefully to distinguish the difference between their own priorities and meeting the needs of others in the family.

O: OCCUPATION

What work occupies their time can tell you about their task and people skills, and whether they operate at a slower or faster pace.

For example:

"What do you enjoy most about your work?" — Listen closely to the answer to this question to determine if they are more outgoing or reserved, and more task or people-oriented.

Answer 1. "I am one of the top salespeople for a major corporation. I have one of the largest territories with the top sales dollars." To handle this type of a position this individual must be outgoing just to get the results. Now you know the person must be in the Outgoing half of the **DISC** circle.

Answer 2. "I am a chemical engineer for a small company. It's not very exciting, but I enjoy it. I just work in the lab most of the day." To do work in a lab all day would require a more reserved type person. You now can move your finger down into the Reserved half of the **DISC** circle.

Answer 3. "I sell directly to the public. I really enjoy helping people. I also get to meet so many very interesting individuals!" This person seems to really enjoy people, which would indicate they are people-oriented.

Answer 4. "I like to say that I am a household engineer. I'm lucky if I manage to engineer a few minutes to do what I want to do in a day! Three children are a lot of work!" This person approaches caring for children as a task. You probably know that you are talking to a task-oriented individual.

Just by listening to a person talk about their occupation you should be able to determine whether a person is Outgoing or Reserved and Task or People-oriented.

R: RECREATION

What they do for relaxation and why they do it may indicate whether they are fast or slower-paced, and whether they enjoy tasks or people more. Look here for a common interest you may share to begin building a relationship.

For example:

"What do you like to do for recreation or as a hobby?" Different types like different diversions for different reasons. Let's listen again to see if they may be Outgoing or Reserved and Task or People-oriented.

Answer 1. "I just love to sit at home on the weekends and read a good book." This person sounds more reserved.

Answer 2. "I can hardly wait until the weekend to go out with my friends. We have a good time whatever we do!" From this simple answer you can safely identify a high *I*, who is Outgoing and People-oriented.

Answer 3. "I compete on the tennis team in our neighborhood. When I don't have to work on an extra work project, I always have a project to finish at home. I like to coach my son's basketball team too." This person is probably outgoing and is more certainly task-oriented.

Answer 4. "Right now I am enjoying a fascinating study of my genealogy. I have traced my ancestors to Switzerland and northern Italy in the nineteenth century!" Only a reserved, task-oriented person would enjoy this kind of free time activity.

One question about recreation or hobbies can yield a wealth of personality information!

The last question explores what types of activities they enjoy to help identify what motivates them. Finding their passion will help you find their style and a bridge to introduce them to the business.

M: MOTIVATOR

What is the reward a person needs for achievement? Is their passion the reward, recognition, achievement, appreciation, correctness, or challenge? Exactly what motivates them to excel?

For example:

"What do you find is your best motivator to help you really work at something? Do you have a dream for the future?" Listen again:

Answer 1. "I would really love to be able to give my children the support they need to complete their education." The word "support" may indicate a high **S** type, especially when their motivator seems to be supporting their family.

Answer 2. "I'm at my best when I go out and make things happen to get results!" Saying that he or she is best at getting results simply shouts a high **D** type!

Answer 3. "I really enjoy seeing things done correctly and carefully. I am most pleased with an excellent job delivered on time." See how quickly you key in to the words "correctly" and carefully"? You may easily recognize this high **C** type.

Answer 4. "I love to get a party going and give people a good time. I dream about being on a stage, meeting my favorite star!" This person shouts high *I*, doesn't she?

Using the FORM technique can not only give you many indications about someone's personality style; it can also help you find a common interest for further conversation.

Almost anyone enjoys talking with someone who is genuinely interested in him or her. Sharing your own short stories about a common interest may open the door of opportunity to begin to build a relationship. Begin to recognize their personality perspective to better work with and communicate with them.

One Diamond tells the story of nudging her husband's leg under the table to get his attention while showing the Plan early in their business. He didn't respond, so she finally kicked him — and their *prospect* yelled out in pain! This is not the kind of communication that you want! You may discover two valuable experiences as you communicate with your spouse about recognizing styles at a glance:

1. You may learn to understand how your spouse thinks, and you may improve your communication skills with each other as you benefit from each other's perceptions — you are helping each other to raise your *Personality Quotient*!

2. Because your spouse's style is probably very different from yours, you may help each other to become more sensitive to the communication styles of others, so that you can prepare your thoughts or feelings to relate to many different people. You may then be able to better concentrate on the needs, desires, and motivations of your prospects and find greater business success!

Clues to Look For

Following is our *Obvious Indicators* chart. You can use this information from two directions: when you see these traits, tendencies and activities in an individual, you may more easily identify the high types in their style. From the opposite direction, when you already know an individual's style, you may predict and prepare for their possible actions and attitudes.

Take a few minutes to explore our **DISC** Obvious Indicators on the following page. Knowing the high types in your style, read the columns that may describe you. If you know your spouse or friend's style, read the columns that may describe them. Watching how someone lives every day will show you some of these obvious indicators. No matter what our personality style may be, each of us has a natural reaction to each of these areas. You may find some surprises hidden in this chart! You may, for the first time, begin to understand how your spouse shops from the Buying Methods! Have fun trying to find a friend who fits into each type!

Someone has said that agriculture is just like farming, except that farming is *doing it*. Until now, this **DISC** information has been an interesting theory. *Doing it* begins with this chapter. You can begin to put it into practice! You want to have the tools to empower yourself to improve your life and business. Now is the time to try the Third Step to raising your **PQ**, *Adapting Your Style to Have Better Relationships*. You can practice communicating more effectively as you recognize styles at a glance and adapt to their needs.

A story is told about a little boy who got into an argument with some kids twice his size. He drew a line in the dirt and dared them to cross it. Without hesitation, they accepted the challenge, whereupon the little guy smiled and said, "Now you're on my side!" That's the goal of applying this information: to bring us from opposing sides to the same side; to become a winning team.

Is this going to be an easy step for you? The first step may feel like folding your hands the wrong way – remember how that felt? Talk with your upline and downline, practice these concepts, and remember that you have been adapting all your life, but now you have the benefit of a pattern that makes sense! Start with the First Step to raise your **PQ** and before you know it, you will be taking this Third Step! "The journey of a thousand miles begins with a single step... and a road map!" Now you have it. You can do it!

Obvious Indicators	D	I	S	C
Buying Method	Decides quickly; prefers new and practical	Decides impulsively, from feeling and appearance	Decides slowly; prefers the traditional	Decides cautiously; prefers the exceptional; likes value
Personal Decor	Large desk, awards, useful accessories	Flashy, trendy, with fun pictures	Family pictures, personal mementos	Aesthetically pleasing, unique, functional
Body Language	Big gestures; leans forward, advancing	Expressive, friendly posture; amusing	Gentle gestures; reassuring	Unemotional, controlled gestures; assessing
Organizational Method	Accessible, practical, not neat	Piles rather than files; disorganized	Systematic, traditional	Highly organized, personalized detailed system
Energizing Recharge	Competition; Physical activity	Interaction; Social activity	Retreat; Undirected activity	Solitude; Cognitive Activity
Speech Patterns	Directive tones, abrupt, interrupting always doing something	Talkative, varied tones, personal, easily distracted	Conversational, warm tones, friendly, prefers listening	Clarifying, monotone, logical, focused, emotionless

A TAKE ACTION

CHAPTER TEN

PERSONAL ACTION PLAN

This is an opportunity to recognize Styles at a Glance.

Question 1: Think of one person in your family. Using the Pointing Technique (pp. 124-125) identify the highest type in their style.

Name _____ has a high _____ style.

Question 2: Using the *Simple Ask* Technique (pp. 125-126) talk to one person today and *Simply Ask* them the two questions in order to identify their personality style.

Name _____ has a high _____ style.

Question 3: Think of a very close friend. Using the FORM Technique (pp. 126-130) describe how you would recognize and identify their style.

I know that my friend, _____ has a high _____ style, because

_____

_____

_____

Contact and Invite with Style

In the Wild West, fortunes were made exploring, searching and panning for gold. In 1841 they began to call it ***prospecting*** because it held a good *prospect*, the anticipation of a valuable possibility for the future – the dream of gold! You do prospecting of a different kind in the business: you search for a good prospect, a candidate to join your business who is equally valuable, a possibility for the future who has the dream of a Diamond! You explore, you search, to contact and invite many different people to find good prospects. Because Diamonds come with all ***DISC*** personality styles, good prospects will not only have your style, but many different styles. The approach that works well with one prospect may not interest a different personality style. We all want to learn how to approach a prospect effectively for their personality style.

LEARN TO BE ATTRACTIVE

Haven't you seen this happen on a beach somewhere? An attractive girl walks down the beach. A few heads turn. Eyes follow her as she passes. Someone whistles. A couple of interested fellows get up and follow her, hoping she will turn and speak to them. She has their attention. They want to get her attention too. What will happen next...? She now has our attention too!

Our story started with a girl who was attractive physically. She was probably born with some natural beauty, and she learned, complementing that natural beauty, how to present herself in a way that others would enjoy. In a similar way, you were born with natural beauty in your personality style. You also can learn how to present yourself, and your business, in a way that is attractive to others.

One Diamond has explained that some Independent Business Owners can be like vultures, as they swoop down on their prospects like a predator on his prey. Can you see how the task-oriented **D** and **C** types might especially tend to do this? Who is attracted to a vulture? Other Independent Business Owners can be like a fluffy puppies, following you everywhere. Anyone loves a puppy to follow them at first, but if they go with you everywhere they soon look more like a shaggy dog that looks a little muddy. They just are not so cute or cuddly anymore. Can you see how people-oriented **I** and **S** types could make prospects feel dogged? If this is such a great opportunity, why would someone be dogging them, begging to get them involved? How attractive is a muddy, shaggy dog?

As you learn to be attractive to others, you present yourself and the business in a way that others will enjoy. You want to draw their interest so that you have their attention. To do this, you must raise your **PQ** as you contact and invite.

How **DISC** Types Will Contact and Invite

The **D** type is determined. They will approach contacting as a task, will keep the goal in mind and will drive forward to accomplish the goal. Rejection will not so easily deter them, because their goal will focus on their number of contacts first, and a rejection is still a contact! They just directly move on to someone else and try again. The **D** type will be more attractive by raising their **PQ** to be more patient with potential prospects who may need time to think before giving them an answer. This high **D** type adapts their naturally decisive style to give time to less decisive styles. People will be attracted to their powerful style and feel that the business is powerful too.

The **I** type, with their fun, friendly style, naturally attracts many people to them. They often can invite someone who will want to come because they recognize another important person whom the high **I** has invited! The **I** type will be more attractive by raising their **PQ** to remember to follow through with commitments to those people and raise their credibility with other more serious styles. This high **I** type adapts their naturally fun-loving style to be more businesslike. People will be attracted to their fun-loving style and feel that the business will be fun for them too.

The **S** type, with their reserved, warm style, will find it naturally hard to make calls to contact and invite people to come to presentation meetings. They would prefer to first get to know someone to comfortably see if the business would really help the other person. The **S** type will be more attractive by raising their **PQ** to simply ask the person by, sharing what they appreciate about the business and asking another person to see for themselves how they would enjoy the business. This high **S** type adapts their stable, reserved style to be more outgoing and assertive. People will be attracted to their stable, warm style and feel that the business will be comfortable for them too.

The **C** type, with their reserved, correct style, will not naturally like to make calls to contact because they want to do it perfectly by the system. They would prefer to explain how the system works instead of engaging in the informal conversation of contacting. The **C** type will be more attractive by raising their **PQ** to talk about how the business has benefited them and invite other styles to explore the benefits. This high **C** type adapts their correct, conscientious style to be more caring and flexible. People will be attracted to their conscientious, careful style and feel that the business will be correct for them too.

How to Contact and Invite the **DISC** Types

We have looked at how the **DISC** personality types learn to be attractive to contact and invite. Now we will explore the way to get the interest and attention of **DISC** personality types as you contact and invite each type.

Contact and Invite the High **D**

Use a direct and bottom line approach with the high **D**. These prospects will be very busy and must be attracted to **what** you have to offer. Tell them just enough of **what** they want to know to get their attention, so they will decide to accept your invitation. Simply tell them that you've got some big things starting to happen, and you want them to be in on the action. Be careful not to find yourself answering too many of their **what** questions, or they may decide that they know **what** to do without coming! As you contact and invite the high **D**, be sure and think in terms of **what** the business will do for them.

Tips to Inviting the High **D** style

- Expect to overcome obstacles
- Focus on action-based results
- Be brief and specific
- Be credible
- Provide challenge and choices
- Get to the bottom line benefits

CONTACT AND INVITE THE HIGH **I**

Use a warm, friendly approach with the high **I**. These prospects will want to talk and will be attracted by your excitement. They will want to talk about **who** they know and **who** might know you, and they seem to know just about everyone! They will do most of the talking, but remember to tell them just enough about **who** they might recognize or **who** will recognize them to get their attention. Be sure to tell them that you have someone you want them to meet! Then they will be excited to accept your invitation. Be careful not to find yourself listening to their stories about too many other things, or they may forget your invitation. As you contact and invite the high **I**, be sure and think in terms of **who** is in the business and the recognition your prospect can receive.

Tips to Inviting the High *I* Style

- Let them express their ideas
- Keep a friendly environment
- Focus on their accomplishments
- Provide recognition for their achievements
- Gently steer them back to business
- Turn talk to action

CONTACT AND INVITE THE HIGH *S*

Use a gentle and unthreatening manner with the high *S*. These prospects will want to get to know you and to know that you have a genuine interest in them. You will need a relationship with them before they will be comfortable exploring *how* the business might benefit them. They will be attracted by your affirmation and appreciation of them, and will slowly be comfortable with accepting your invitation. Be sure to tell them *how* friendly the people in your group really are. Tell them just enough of *how* they will appreciate the business to get their attention so they will decide to accept your invitation. Be careful not to find yourself answering too many of their *how* questions, or they may be overwhelmed with *how* much change is possible, and withdraw without coming! As you contact and invite the high *S*, be sure and think in terms of *how* the business is a friendly team that needs their support.

Tips to Inviting the High *S* style

- Be warm, agreeable and unthreatening
- Talk slowly and do not rush them
- Give them time to adjust to new ideas
- Show appreciation for their interest
- Demonstrate sincerity
- Provide follow-up support

Contact and Invite the High C

Use a factual approach and unemotional manner with the high **C**. These prospects will be very cautious and will want to know **why** you are interested in them. Tell them just enough of **why** they would benefit, to get their attention, so they will decide to accept your invitation. Be sure to tell them that there will be people at the meeting who can answer the questions that they will want to ask. Be careful not to find yourself answering too many of their **why** questions, or they may get lost in the details before coming! As you contact and invite the high **C**, be sure and think in terms of **why** the business is a credible, calculated opportunity for them.

Tips to Inviting the High C style

- Check your facts
- Show how they fit in
- Avoid emotional appeal
- Answer questions carefully
- Be specific on points of agreement
- Show a "pro & con" balance sheet
- Provide proof

Understanding personality styles gives you an idea what to expect from a prospect in a conversation. You have also begun to understand how your personality style communicates. Take a few minutes to read the chart on the next page. Read each column to understand the predictable patterns of each type. Then, perhaps you might like to read each row to see how **DISC** types can be different in so many ways! These clues may help you understand how your prospect may approach your conversation. Use it as a reference before contacting or inviting.

Predictable Patterns	D	I	S	C
Wants to know:	What?	Who?	How?	Why?
Wants you to be:	Direct	Excited	Sincere	Credible
Dreams of:	Accomplish-ments, money	Being a star	Security for family	Long-term profit
Processes information by asking:	What will work?	Is it fun?	Give me time?	Is it logical?
Driven by:	Will	Feelings	Trust	Intellect
Key strength:	Firm	Fun	Friendly	Factual
Key struggle:	To be friendly	To be factual	To be firm	To be fun
Secret to their success:	To be under authority	To be more credible	To be more decisive	To be more caring
Motivating statement:	You're the one in charge	You're the greatest	You're so dependable	You are a good thinker
Killer statement:	You don't matter!	You think that's funny?	You let me down!	You made a mistake!

Reporting on Raising our *PQ* as We Contact and Invite

Just as any good reporter must cover the five W's, you can use this little key to remember to raise your *PQ* as you contact and invite. Remember *What* with the **high D** type. Emphasize *Who* with the **high I** type. Explain *How* with the **high S** type. Recall *Why* with the **high C** type. Now, *Where* do you start? You start with a conversation, and each personality type has different strengths and struggles with conversations. Your upline has proven methods of opening conversations for meeting people and bringing up the benefits of your business. We recommend that you ask them what works best — we'll bet it starts with being friendly... As the old Jewish proverb says, "Don't open a shop unless you know how to smile."

One thing you will quickly find: simply saying "Hi..." or "It sure is cold today..." is not a conversational icebreaker because it doesn't really require any interaction. A stranger's mumbled back response of "Hello..." or "Sure is..." isn't going to take your conversation anywhere.

Let s Play Catch!

Thinking of conversation as a game of catch may even help more reserved styles to enjoy interaction with another person. How do you play catch? First, you need at least two players. One starts with the ball, throwing it to the other player. The other player catches the ball, then throws it back to the first player. The game continues as long as the person who catches the ball throws it again. In a conversation, the first player throws the ball by asking a question.

Learning How to Ask Questions

There are two kinds of questions. The first kind of question is the closed-ended question, called the closed probe. This is a question that solicits a "yes" or "no" response, or a very short answer, like a number. A closed probe would be right to use in the final stages of asking someone if they would like to join our business team. When you want to start a conversation, or find out more about a person, using a closed probe is like holding the ball!

The second kind of question is the open-ended question, called the open probe. Generally the words "who, what, when, where, how, and why" are used somewhere in these questions. You have seen these words already as communication tips for *D*, *I*, *S*, and *C* types! Try to use these words when asking questions of their respective types. The answers from open probe questions are more involved. Using this kind of question is like throwing the ball – you can expect the other player to throw the ball back to you! Their answers will uncover your prospect's wants, needs, desires, and dreams. Something they say to you should help you to relate benefits of your business, and you can explore this idea as you talk. Don't forget to keep using open probes in your game of catch! Soon you will find another member for your business team!

Closed Probes	Open Probes
Are you...?	Who...?
Do/Did/Don't you...?	What...?
Is/Isn't...?	Where...?
Can/Could/Would...?	When...?
Has/Have you...?	How...?
Will you...?	Why...?
Shall you...?	Which...?

THE ART OF ASKING QUESTIONS

Asking questions comes easily for outgoing styles, while more reserved styles may need a more specific plan for effectively asking questions. An IBO must develop an effective method of fact-finding to produce information that will reveal the prospect's situation. Try different questions until you find a few that are comfortable for you. They should arise naturally in the conversation. To be effective, it is also important to listen to what your prospect is telling you. Listening will come more easily for more reserved styles than for outgoing styles. Listening will give you the information necessary to prepare for showing the Plan to this prospect. Outgoing styles may need a more specific plan for effectively listening for important and useful information.

Caution: Avoid cross examination! Most people will resent being interrogated. They need to understand that you are truly interested in them and that you are open about the reason for your question. A developing, positive relationship is the best reason for any question. Do not manipulate your prospect! Using a variety of questions that are sensitive to the person's style will allow you to direct the conversation to vital information and leave the prospect feeling satisfied that this was a friendly conversation, not an interrogation.

 Remember, an open probe will open up great conversations!

An open-ended question is also the best way to direct a conversation. Can you direct the conversation with a question? We believe you can. This is contrary to the normal response that tries to take control by talking more. A two-year old gains total control of a parent by asking "why" all the time. Every time the parent asks the child to do something, the child asks "why." This totally neutralizes the request of the adult. We can learn a lesson from this two-year old!

The next time you find yourself losing direction in a conversation for contacting or inviting, pause and ask an open probe. You will be surprised how quickly you will be back in control of the conversation and you will also be finding out some important information. Warning: When you do get your prospect talking, remember to be quiet and listen! As you listen, you may also think about your next move.

We have found that people respond well to inquiries about themselves, or to a request for assistance. You might start a conversation with a stranger by starting with a complimentary question: "That's a great necktie — I'm looking for one like that. Where did you get it?" Or, "Excuse me... could you help me...?" Regardless of personality styles, when you ask this question, most people will respond positively. With either of these questions, the next logical step is to extend you hand

and say, "I'm sorry. I didn't introduce myself. My name is..." Consider this way to start your conversational game of catch!

What if you have caught the conversation ball (it is your turn to speak) and you are still not sure how to throw it back, what to say? Ask the person an interesting, open probe question about himself or herself; and when practical, weave in a sincere compliment, like this:

- **What** do you do for a living? (Open Probe)
- That has always interested me — please tell me more about... (Open Probe)
- **How** long have you been doing that? (Open Probe)
- **Why** did you get started in it? (Open Probe)
- You must be an expert then — **what** do you like best about it? (Open Probe)
- **Who** might I know who does this, too? (Open Probe)

By the time you have listened to all the answers to these open probes you will have learned a great deal about your prospect. Everyone wants to feel important, and we want to feel that we are really good at doing something. The following questions seem to help get the prospect talking.

- **How** would you like to spend the next ten years?
- In four or five years, **what** would you consider to be a really good income?
- Doing what you are now doing, **how** long will it take you to reach that income level?
- If you had all the time you wanted and money wasn't a problem, **what** kinds of things would you like to be doing?
- **Who** would you like to spend some extra time with?
- **Why** do you feel that would be important for you?

One of the benefits of asking your prospect questions, that is often overlooked, is that it builds rapport with that prospect. Many of us make a subconscious judgment at the end of a conversation as to how well the person listened to us. Typically this judgment is based on who did the most talking.

Focusing your questions on them, listen to their responses. Share a little bit of yourself, too, and people will tell you the most amazing things about themselves! Without much searching, you can uncover specific needs in their lives that can be met by the benefits of your business. They will think you are a brilliant conversationalist if you become a brilliant listener!

Zig Ziglar tells the story of a lady who sat next to Great Britain's Prime Minister, William Gladstone, at a formal state dinner. They talked throughout the evening. Several evenings later, the same lady sat with Great Britain's other legendary Prime Minister, Benjamin Disraeli. Someone asked her what the main difference was between these two great leaders. She said that after her conversation with Mr. Gladstone, she was convinced he was the most brilliant man England had ever produced. However, after spending her evening with Mr. Disraeli, she was convinced that she, herself, was one of the brightest, wittiest, most knowledgeable people that England had ever produced. Many articles about Disraeli also document his skill with people. What was Disraeli's secret? Disraeli himself said, "Talk to a man about himself and he will listen for hours." Zig Ziglar says that every person wears this invisible sign: MAKE ME FEEL IMPORTANT!

LEARNING HOW TO LISTEN

In your conversational game of catch, asking the open probe question is like tossing the ball. If you made a good throw, the other player will catch the ball and throw it back! Now it is your turn to catch the ball. Catching the ball is like listening to the answer to your question. You wait in expectation, but you don't know what is coming until the other player actually throws the ball! When you ask questions, listen to the answers! Remember to receive both the person and the person's response to communicate that this person is important to you.

Several years ago, Dr. Paul Rankin of The Ohio State University, conducted two identical studies to identify communication skills used on a daily basis. Both studies produced the same results:

Seven of every 19 waking minutes, we are communicating in these ways:

70% of our waking hours are spent communicating in these ways:

Writing	9%
Reading	16%
Speaking	30%
Listening	45%

Formal education or training teaches communication in these ways:

Writing	Up to 16 years
Reading	Up to 12 years
Speaking	6 to 8 years
Listening	0 to 1 year
Learning to listen	0 years

Although listening is the most common communication factor, learning to listen is not directly taught! Listening is a very important skill for the IBO. Effective listening allows you to communicate with your prospect. An objection cannot be overcome if you fail to hear it correctly. A sale may be lost when you miss a buying signal. Listening skills need to be developed and practiced daily for you to become an effective IBO. Begin now to notice your own listening practices.

If you are *an outgoing, fast-paced person*, you have probably been distracted in the middle of a conversation. Many different things are going on all around you while you are talking with someone. Your eyes keep wandering from your friend to what is happening nearby. You pick up snatches of passing conversations. One thing reminds you of another, and your mind goes racing in other directions. Mentally, you drift in and out of the most important conversation — the one in which you are personally participating! Keeping your eyes focused on the person with whom you are speaking, will help you to focus your attention on your conversation. This takes practice. Remember, as a kid, when you were having a great time playing catch, and the other kid just abruptly took his ball and went home? That nagging feeling of disappointment, even distrust, is easy to remember, even now. Focusing on your own conversation will keep you from leaving a prospect with that same nagging feeling of disappointment and distrust.

If you are *a reserved, slower-paced person*, you have probably been in the middle of trying to invite someone to a meeting, when they seem to lose interest in the conversation and wander off or politely make an excuse to leave. You may have hesitated to say something, or have spoken so quietly because you were unsure of yourself or what you wanted to say. Mentally, you may be arguing with yourself or your mind has gone blank, but verbally you leave the other person feeling confused. This is similar to the child who sees a more popular child approaching while he is playing catch with a friend. He thinks the popular child will take his friend off to do something else. In his confusion, the first child just stands and rolls the ball from hand to hand. His friend is also confused by this, and thinks he doesn't want to play anymore. He goes off to find something else to do. Be familiar with what you plan to say, and then say it with confidence, so that your prospect will not be confused and wander away from the conversation.

Remember the game of conversational catch. Use it to attract, contact and invite according to your style and the style of your prospect! Use your Franklin® Planner to record the important details of your conversation so that you can recall them when you need them. What did this person tell you about their dreams, what really motivates them, what were their children's names, etc...? If you depend on your memory and make a mistake about that child named Tarzan you will lose credibility. You may soon have so many prospects that writing it down is the only way you can remember!

Telling the Story to Attract your Prospects

An important part of storytelling is learning to get your listener involved with your characters and to build anticipation for the conclusion of the story. Telling the story of your business needs to do this, too. You make a contact and begin to tell the story according to their personality style so that they get involved with you and your story. You develop your story to build anticipation so that when you extend the invitation to your business they cannot wait to say yes! To illustrate this storytelling, we will use a story involving the respected and famous Jimmy Stewart. He earned our respect and love with his fabulous acting and exemplary personal life. In the classic Christmas tale, *It's a Wonderful Life,* the story begins with a scene that really attracts our attention.

> *Jimmy Stewart, as George Bailey, stares at the freezing water beneath a snowy bridge where he stands shivering, ready to jump to end his miserable, worthless life. Before George can jump, someone else plunges into the turbulent water. Immediately George jumps into the dangerous current and drags an old man safely to the river's edge.*

If we have begun our story well, you are involved now with George and the old man. You are attracted to the story and wonder what will happen next. Notice at this point that we have not told you many things. You do not know why George wants to die. You know nothing about the old man except that he is old, wet, and cold. But we have your attention.

> *When the two men make their way to the bridge house, to warm themselves by the stove, their conversation reveals to us that the old man, named Clarence, is really an angel. He has been sent to help George see how important his life really is, and to earn his angel wings by doing this. Clarence un-*

successfully tries to talk George into understanding the value of his life. George cannot be persuaded. As Clarence listens, George laments what a hopeless mess his life is, and he wishes that he had never been born. Clarence decides that making his wish come true may be the only way that Clarence will get his wish, his angel wings. Clarence tells George that he has his wish: George has never been born. George bolts out into the cold, black night, confused and angry.

As more details of our character's dilemma unfold, we begin to understand his feelings and his frustration. We also begin to care about him, and to hope that he can find a reason to live. Notice that we really do not know enough to predict what that reason will be, but we hope that he can find it. This is similar to sharing with your contact about their current frustrations and unfulfilled dreams, and the hope that there may be a way out of this situation.

In the dimly lit, snowy street, George staggers to old, familiar places and finds, to his growing horror, that these terrible places are not familiar to him any longer, and the people he knows in these places do not know him. He wildly tries to convince these people that they do know him, and frantically grabs Clarence to choke some answers out of him. George is ready to listen.

Our interest in understanding the resolution to the story is now very high. We like George, and we feel that Clarence should tell him, and us, what is really going on. This is the point in your business story where your prospect wants to listen, so you can begin to share what your business story means to you.

Clarence begins to show us what has really happened. George is always helping others, often through his own sacrifice. Someone else's careless mistake, about which he has not known, robs him of the money he needs to pay a debt. This unpaid debt is due to a greedy, selfish old lender who cannot wait to take the little bit of security George has. This is the impending disaster that drove him to the snowy bridge. As Clarence continues to tell George's story to us, George begins to remember all the special gifts he has shared with his wonderful family and friends. He decides that he wants to live, and that he wants to go home.

We are satisfied that, despite the misfortune that awaits him, George has achieved his fondest dreams in the loving relationships he finds at home. This is the point in your business story to share with your prospect how your business has helped you fulfill your dreams, and to suggest that the business may help him too.

George returns home to find his house bursting with family and friends who have sacrificially given, just as George had given to them in the past, and have together collected enough money to pay his debt. George is overwhelmed, and, gratified by their care for him, he declares, "It's a wonderful life!" George has his life back, and Clarence also gets his wings!

Just like any good story, everyone lives happily ever after! As you practice telling your business story, your conclusion will help you reach your dreams, too. Your prospect will be attracted by you to your business and together your dreams can come true!

Contacting and inviting are a lot like our story, too. Here are a few points to consider from *It's a Wonderful Life*:

1. Clarence met George (his prospect) where he was — in his real life situation.
2. Clarence got George's attention by jumping in the water.
3. Clarence opened a conversation with George.
4. Clarence used open probe questions to understand George's needs.
5. Clarence offered a solution based on George's personality style.
6. Clarence walked with George along the path to the answer.
7. Clarence was there to give George his life back when George finally decided that his life did make a difference.
8. Clarence (high *I*) must have understood George's personality style because he never pushed George too hard. Clarence supportively met George's High *S* needs and answered his questions in a caring way.

Mark Twain once observed, "The difference between the right word and the almost right word is the difference between lightning and a lightning bug." The most effective way to tell your business story will develop as you practice it. When you find the "right" words, you will feel at ease, and so will your prospect. The best way to start, we can tell you from the experience of many successful Independent Business Owners, is to write it down! This clarifies what you really want to say. If you woke one of these successful IBOs from a sound sleep, they would probably be able to tell their story on the spot because they have planned it and rehearsed it until it is naturally their own.

DON T GET DISCOURAGED

Almost 60 years ago, prospector Rafael Solano sat discouraged and exhausted on a boulder in a dry South American riverbed. "I'm through," he announced to his three companions. "There's no use going on any longer. See this pebble?" He picked up a stone. "It makes about 999,999 I've picked up and not a diamond so far. If I pick up another, it will be a million — but what's the use? I'm quitting."

The men had spent months in Venezuela prospecting, searching for diamonds, stooping, gathering pebbles, hoping for a single sign of a diamond. They thought about giving up, but Solano finally said, "I quit!" One of the other men responded, "So... pick up another and make it a million."

"All right," Solano agreed. He stooped down, digging with his hand into a pile of stones. He pulled out a single stone. It was almost the size of a hen's egg. "Here it is," he announced, "the last one." For that one-in-a-million pebble, New York jeweler Harry Winston paid Rafael Solano $200,000. It became known as *The Liberator*, and it was the largest diamond ever found up to that time. And it was just one more stone.

Natural *DISC*ouragement

Ds may quickly become discouraged and want to quit when they don't sign up as many prospects as they have set for a goal.

*I*s may take the prospects' rejection personally, since they want everyone to come to their party and like them.

*S*s will fail to bring the prospect to a decision on becoming a part of the business, even while they may be personally helpful and supportive.

*C*s will be frustrated, thinking that the prospects just did not understand all the important information that they know about the business.

How *DISC* Types Raise Their *PQ* to Lower Their *DISC*OURAGEMENT

*D*s remember that they always set high goals, but also realize that they have achieved a great deal.

*I*s remind themselves that just because a prospect rejects the business opportunity, they have not rejected them. It simply means that the prospect may not be ready for this concept at this time.

*S*s remind themselves that they can best help their friends by sharing the business with them. They know how much the business has helped them, and that it can help their friends too.

*C*s remember that feelings and other factors may hinder their prospect from choosing to come into the business. The information they have given is still valid and may be valuable to the prospect in another way or at another time.

Regardless of your personality style, you will experience some disappointments as you prospect for people to listen to your business story. At times, you may feel that you are wasting the relatively small amount of money you are spending in advertising, contacting, and inviting prospects. This is an area where you should talk honestly with your upline leaders. Because of their experience, they can help you be more effective.

Recently, a Diamond shared this idea: Among 100 people you might approach, there is a bell curve of acceptance. About 10 people will say "yes" just because you ask them to look at the business. On the other end of the curve, there are probably as many people who will say "no" for exactly the same reason — if you are for it, they are against it! Then, in the middle, there are about 80 people who may be willing to consider your business idea. They will approach it with a more or less open mind and are willing to be persuaded. On which group should you concentrate your attention?

You probably would not want to waste time on the negative ten. You might be tempted to go with the positive ten, the "yes" people who tend to go along with whatever you are doing. These ten are the most likely just to sign an application. They might never even buy a tube of Glister® from their own business! Put your energies into the middle group of 80, with the highest capacity for success.

Among the 100 people you might approach, how can you know which of the 100 people these 80 people are? There is only one way: you simply ask them! This really is what contacting and inviting are all about: making friends and simply asking them if they want to become a part of your business.

JUST DO IT

Arthur Priebe, a great insurance salesman, used to suffer from an affliction he called *doorknob-a-phobia*. A common affliction, this fear of rejection has also caused many Independent Business Owners to hesitate, when they could have moved ahead. The advice Arthur Priebe gave his colleagues will be especially helpful to the more reserved **S**s and **C**s. He suggested that the timid salesmen hold this debate with themselves:

"Where am I?"

"I'm in the hall."

"Where do I want to be?"

"I want to be in that man's office."

"What will happen if I turn the doorknob and go inside?"

"The worst that could happen is I'd be thrown back into the hall."

"Well, that's where I am now, so what have I got to lose?"

What is the worst that can happen when you approach someone with your wonderful business opportunity? They could say *no*. Unless you *simply ask*, you will never know what they might say! If they say *no*, at least you can cross them off your list and move on! Surveys that have been conducted among many leaders show an average of a thousand Plans are shown on the way to becoming a Diamond. One thousand is much less than one million! Just one more, and this could be the one...

If You Still Struggle with What You Should Say...

Does it seem that all of your polite, innocent conversation goes well until you try to change gears and introduce your business? Try this:

Dialog:

Prospect asks — "What do you do?"

You answer— "I own my own business... How about you?"

*Prospect answers—*Very often, they will tell you where they work or what job they hold — but then, they will return to you with a magic question:

Prospect asks —"What kind of business do you own?"

At a time when so many people are thinking about one day having a business of their own, your response creates curiosity.

There are many things you might say that could encourage a prospect to question you further. One leader says that you should be able to tell someone what you are all about, in 25 words or less. Your upline can recommend a specific approach for you and coach you as you practice it. This will become your business mission statement. Depending on what you have observed about your prospect's style, and depending on the comfort level of your own style, you might choose to respond casually along these lines:

You answer — "I help people build secondary incomes that don't depend on their ability to show up for work every day..."

or

— "I set up home-based businesses that allow people to spend quality time together as a family..."

or

— "Have you seen how many television and magazine ads have website addresses at the bottom? Well, we have figured out a way to cash in on the growing internet shopping business...

or

— "I help people start their own business and become their own boss..."

or

— "I let customers bypass the stores and shopping centers and have their consumables automatically delivered right to their door..."

or

— "I help people of any age create profits they can use in retirement, rather than hoping Social Security will still be around..."

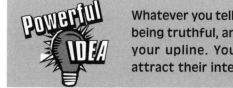

Whatever you tell your prospect, be sure you are being truthful, and work it out beforehand with your upline. You don't have to say much to attract their interest for more information:

Prospect asks — "That sounds interesting. How do you do that?"

This is a vulnerable spot where we need to guard our speech and our emotions. It is true that whatever seems to be freely available has diminished value, so whatever you say, make it attractive and don't pounce on people. You might say something like...

You answer — "It's interesting that you should ask. Actually, I'm in the process of expanding my business, and maybe you could help me with that. See, I'm looking for a... sharp, enthusiastic person — do you know someone who fits that description..."

or

— "It is a proven system that has a predictable outcome for people who are willing to learn and are serious about their future..."

or

— "I am working a system that allows us to do business all over the world from our phones and personal computers..."

Another practical issue: what do you say if your prospect asks, "Is it *Amway*?" It is important to think this through ahead of time, so that when the question comes up, you are able to give a solid, appropriate response based on your personality style and the style of your prospect.

With a low **PQ** the natural response is:

Ds defend themselves by becoming confrontational.

Is defend themselves by becoming glib and misleading.

Ss defend themselves by trying to withdraw.

Cs defend themselves logically against anything that seems like an attack on their intelligence or integrity.

With a raised **PQ** the response is:

Ds would first stop themselves from being confrontational and hold their direct response. Thinking about the prospect's style, they would ask this open probe question, "What do you know about Amway?" They allow the prospect to talk while they listen.

Is would hold their wordy response. They simply ask the question and let the prospect talk. Thinking about the prospect's style, they ask, "What do you know about Amway?" They allow the prospect to talk while they listen.

Ss would resolve to stay calm and would repeat this helpful response. Thinking about their prospect's style they would ask this question, "What do you know about Amway?" They allow the prospect to talk while they listen.

Cs would hold their information and find out why the prospect has asked the question so that they can give a proper answer. Thinking about their prospect's style they would ask, "What do you know about Amway?" They allow the prospect to talk while they listen.

In each case, the open probe question each style asks is the same: *"What do you know about Amway?"* Many Diamonds have told us this is the best response because it gives the prospect the opportunity to explain what they know or feel, and what they want to know. When you understand how they feel and what they want to know, you can satisfy their need to know with a quality answer.

RAISING YOUR *PQ* AS YOU CONTACT AND INVITE

Remember *What* with the **high D** type.

Emphasize *Who* with the **high I** type.

Explain *How* with the **high S** type.

Recall *Why* with the **high C** type.

Now, *Where* do you start? Start with being friendly... Remember what the proverb says, "Don't open a shop unless you know how to smile."

When is the time to start?

The best time to start is NOW!

CHAPTER ELEVEN

PERSONAL ACTION PLAN

Question 1: Name one thing that you can do to practice becoming more "personality attractive" as you contact and invite.

_____

Question 2: Name the open probe questions and show which **DISC** type goes with each one.

Ask the **D** type *W* _____

Ask the **I** type *W* _____

Ask the **S** type *H* _____

Ask the **C** type *W* _____

Question 3: In twenty-five words or less, write what your business is all about. Be as simple and specific as you know how to be. Then practice telling this business mission statement to three people in your organization._____

_____

_____

Question 4: May we share with you our business mission statement at Personality Insights, Inc?
We teach people to understand themselves and others, in order to have better relationships and build better teams.

This is what we want to do for you!

Show the Plan with Style

Showing the Plan with style is sharing the dream! One of the most enjoyable aspects of this business is sharing your dreams with others and learning about their dreams. Showing the Plan is sharing with someone how this business has empowered you to achieve what is personally important to you, to an extent that you never thought possible. This is what it means to make a dream become a reality! The thought that you can help someone achieve their dreams should excite all of us to show the Plan as often as possible. The more often you show the Plan, the more quickly you will achieve your dreams too!

At functions people often ask, "What is different about Showing the Plan *with Style*?" Showing the Plan *with Style* means raising your **PQ**, adapting your style to meet your prospect's needs as you Show the Plan. At this point in our book, you are taking Step One, *Understanding Yourself*, and Step Two, *Understanding Another Person*. These steps create a growing awareness that you can take Step Three, *Adapting Yourself to Their Needs*, and this is what we do as we Show the Plan *with Style*! Your upline has a system for Showing the Plan; we want to show you that adapting your approach, especially how you say things, does not change the Plan at all. It simply makes you communicate more effectively! Your knowledge and application of personality insights will empower you to Show the Plan with *real* Style.

Showing the Plan with Style in a group presentation means taking the time to include statements that will appeal to each personality type. All **DISC** types will usually be listening when you present the Plan to a group. Using a varied pace, sometimes faster, sometimes more slowly, will keep their attention best. Being very excited and visual as you introduce a concept, but also very careful and accurate as you explain the details will increase your credibility. Progressing efficiently to a strong conclusion will generally get your best results. Draw information from the suggestions for each of the **DISC** types to raise your **PQ** for your group presentations.

Showing the Plan to a couple or an individual gives you the opportunity to adjust your presentation to specific individuals' needs and personality styles. And adjusting your style as you Show the Plan is what this chapter is all about.

TWO DIFFERENT PERSPECTIVES

In Chapter Four, we discussed how each type has a different focus as they approach the business. You and your prospect will usually have different personality styles, so you will naturally have different focuses as you process information. You will also have different life experiences and priorities. What you feel is important in the Plan may be of lesser importance to your prospect. Think about the different focuses that different personality styles may have:

D types are dominant, outgoing and task-oriented, and tend to be direct, fast-paced people. They respond well to people who make their point and give them an opportunity to make choices or meet a challenge. They love to solve problems and make decisions to get results. They respond poorly to people who ramble or offer limited options. They do not like following orders, but would prefer to give orders.

I types are inspiring, outgoing and people-oriented, and tend to be impulsive, fast-paced people. They respond well to people who seem to be lighthearted and make them feel involved in the fun or included in the excitement. They love to receive recognition in a group and approval from people. They respond poorly to people who seem dry and impersonal or cut them off abruptly. They do not like being excluded or dismissed as superficial.

S types are supportive, reserved and people-oriented, and tend to be sweet, slower-paced people. They respond well to people who are reassuring and who give them time to warm up to an idea. They love to take a supportive role where someone else starts and receives the attention of others while they help that person by completing the project. They respond poorly to people who push them to make decisions or to assume high-profile visibility. They do not like rapid change or being taken for granted.

C types are cautious, reserved and task-oriented, and tend to be conscientious, slower-paced people. They respond well to people who are factual and provide statistical backup for any claims or statements they might make. They love to explore ideas and validate concepts. They respond poorly to people who attempt to convince them from an emotional viewpoint or invade their personal space. They do not like spontaneity or illogical responses.

TARGET YOUR PLAN

Different aspects of the business appeal to different personality styles. While one feature may have natural benefits that attract one individual, those same benefits may be of little interest to another. What appeals to one may actually repel another!

Think about this for a moment. Would you casually walk up to a lean, mean Doberman pinscher and put your hand out to pet him? Probably not. However, if a French Poodle bounced up to you wagging his tail, jumping up and down, wiggling all over, happy and excited, would you feel better and safer to reach out to and and pet him? Surely you would! Why? Because you had observed something about his behavior, or temperament, or personality style. You might want the Doberman to guard your home, but that defensive behavior style would make you hesitate to be friendly with a strange dog. The Poodle's friendly behavior would probably make you more comfortable with giving him a friendly little pat on his head. People are just as predictable. If you take the time to observe their behaviors, you will immediately get things started on a better, more positive note. Adapting yourself to approach different people in ways that are beneficial to them will greatly increase your effectiveness, as well as your personal productivity.

Although all features of the Plan can be of benefit to all personality types, the *presentation* will be different because it will emphasize different benefits. How do you adjust your presentation to be more effective in showing the Plan? Turn the page!

SHOWING THE PLAN TO A HIGH *D* TYPE

The high *D*s may be the most difficult type to which you will Show the Plan. The *D* will want to be in control and will challenge you on most every point that you make. Be encouraged, for if you can survive the experience, the *D* type will use that same drive to develop their business with you! They tend to think that building a powerful, independent business is a great idea. In Dr. Rohm's presentation, *Sponsor with Style!*, he shares:

10 TECHNIQUES THAT TARGET THE *D* TYPE'S PREFERENCES WHEN SHOWING THE PLAN:

Emphasize opportunity—be credible.

This is an incredible business opportunity! Be armed with a powerful presentation of success they can achieve. Expect them to challenge your facts, not to get more information, but to see if you really know and believe in what you are showing them.

Be efficient and businesslike.

Treat the dream session as less of a "what would you do if..." discussion and more like a "what will you do when you succeed..." discussion.

Clarify goals.

Show the kind of short-term return that can be realized, and then let them see the longer-term results that will come with dedication and hard work. Be direct in presenting the people and products, as part of the Plan.

Focus on meetings, activities, & showing the Plan.

Show them that each activity has a purpose, and that as they do each one they control the results. Their hard work will pay off in this business!

Don't waste time.

Do not shortchange their dream, and don't let them pressure you into giving them just the bare bones of the Plan — but **be good, be quick, be gone!**

Look at the bottom line.

Show what great potential the business has for them and what others have achieved; then ask them what other vehicle they have to achieve these results within the same time frame.

Be prepared and organized.

Know your materials and be able to explain them powerfully and briefly.

Ask questions about their business operation.

If they have achieved success in their current occupation or business concern, show interest in what they have done and ask how they did it. Use this information about them to tell them that you know they would be successful in this business!

Solve problems and objections.

Show the time efficiency and financial return that can create freedom — again, ask if they have anything else that will fulfill their goals within this time frame. Do not be afraid to say, "I understand your concern. Can we explore the options for this together? You may help us solve that problem."

Review the power in our distribution network.

Present your upline as a powerful business builder with whom they can work, and talk about how they can be a big achiever in your organization.

One thing is sure, showing the Plan to a high **D** will be a challenge! Now that you have a general idea of their perspective, be sure to consider your own style too. If you have a High **D** style, you will naturally present the Plan in a manner consistent with the preferences above. How will this relate to another **D**, an influencing **I**, a supportive **S**, or a critical thinking **C**? When two or more personalities are involved, we call this a Combination. The following chart will better assist you in understanding the high **D** type in Combination with the other types.

If You are a **D**
Remember to Pace Your Presentation
to Their Style

D showing...a D

Emphasize the opportunity

Look at the bottom line

Be businesslike

D showing...an I

Emphasize
successful people
in the business

Look at the recognition
they can achieve

Be more friendly

D showing...an S

Emphasize
upline support

Look at reliability

Be personable

D showing...a C

Emphasize validating materials

Look at hard data

Be patient and logical

Showing the Plan to a High *I* Type

The high *I*s may be the most fun type to which you will Show the Plan! The *I* will want to talk with you to enjoy your attention and gain your approval. If you can keep the high *I* on track, he or she will be excited and want to tell you a story about many of the things you share with them. Be encouraged, for if you can direct the experience, the *I* type will use that same enthusiasm to develop their business with you! They tend to think that building a business with so many people is a great idea. In Dr. Rohm's presentation, *Sponsor with Style*, he shares:

10 Techniques that Target the *I* Type's Preferences when Showing the Plan:

Use testimonials.

Real life stories help them envision their future success. Use the Amagram to show them pictures of real people. This will get them excited about who they can know!

Be friendly.

Smile, relax and enjoy your conversation; show interest in their experiences. It is important to the high *I* for you to enjoy being with them!

Let them talk.

Understand that the high *I* naturally *thinks out loud* when talking about something. If they are not talking at all, you have lost them! The trick for you will be to let them talk, but not let them divert the whole conversation away from showing the Plan.

Don't dwell on details.

They will lose interest if you go into details like the bonus schedule, and will only skim the SA-4400, so focus on how the circles work first. Apply all the incomes to their dreams!

Be enthusiastic.

Say things like "Wouldn't it be fun if we could..." Follow this phrase with several positive pictures of the success that you envision in working with them, and then ask, "Can you see us...?" Enjoy their answers!

Drop names.

Paint an exciting picture of your upline leaders, function speakers, and others in a way that your high *I* prospect will want to meet them — and be known by them.

Provide recognition for their achievements.

Show delight in what they have done so far, and how those achievements will help them move ahead in the business. Recognize especially their ability to learn and warmly present the business.

Show approval.

Let them know you like them! Show them that you want them to have the success and recognition they can find in this business.

Support their dreams.

Enthusiastically enter into painting their dream pictures with them and emphasize how excited you are going to be when you have helped them attain their dreams.

Use their own words, and quote them back.

Listen for phrases that mean a lot to them and use them in your feedback to them. "I heard you say..." They will hear you more effectively because they feel you recognize, understand and accept them.

One thing is sure, showing the Plan to a high *I* will be great fun! Now that you have a general idea of their perspective, be sure to consider your own style too. If you are a High *I*, you will naturally present the Plan in a manner consistent with the preferences above. How will this relate to another *I*, a driving *D*, a supportive *S*, or a critical thinking *C*? When two or more personalities are involved, we call this a Combination. The following chart will better assist you in understanding the high *I* type in Combination with the other types.

If You are an *I*
Remember to Put Facts in Your Fun Presentation!

D

Emphasize real results

Look at meetings and activities

Be prepared with bottom-line facts

I showing...a D

Emphasize approval of their dreams

Look at real people in the business

Be aware of your Plan

I showing...an I

I showing...an S

Emphasize security of the system

Look at how you could help them

Be more patient with them

I showing...a C

Emphasize quality materials

Look at conservative expectations

Be sincerely confident

Showing the Plan to a High **S** Type

The high **S**s may be the most pleasant type to which you will to Show the Plan. The **S** will want to be with you as you gently present the Plan. They will not challenge you, but will need time to think about the support you offer in the business. Be encouraged, for if you can be patient in the experience, the **S** type will use that same steadiness to develop their business with you! They tend to think that building a team through a proven Plan for business is a practical idea. In Dr. Rohm's presentation, *Sponsor with Style*, he shares:

10 Techniques that Target the **S** Type's Preferences when Showing the Plan:

Provide reassurance.

They are not comfortable making quick decisions, so help them see that the Plan is a process and you will want them to be comfortable with the business as they go through this process. Reassure them that they can come to you at any time when they have a question or need assistance.

Ask for their help and show appreciation.

Ask that they help you by asking questions as you present the Plan. Questions that they may have will need to be answered for others too, so let them know that you appreciate their questions.

Stress the security of building the business by the system.

Show them the proven Plan for success in the business, and the reliability and responsiveness of the Corporation to Independent Business Owners and customers. Emphasize how you will assist them personally.

Explain the Plan more completely.

They need to feel that they have had time to process the information and understand it to their satisfaction. Let them know that you want them to be satisfied with the process through which you are taking them.

Show how family members will receive benefits.

Ask them about their family and take time to affirm how important their family is to them. Gently ask them to explore issues that involve their spouse, their parents, or their children. Talk about the importance of time together, retirement and security, future college costs, or a comfortable home to find the need they might like to meet with the business. Show them that the business can be a profitable extension of the network they already share with friends, neighbors, and family. Emphasize that together, everyone benefits.

Pace yourself.

Make your pace meet theirs, because it is very important that they feel comfortable. If they ask if you would like something to drink, say yes! Allow them to share with you so that you can share with them.

Give examples.

Your own positive personal experiences with the corporation and with your upline will be a proven example of the security and stability of the business.

Help them see that their decision is right.

Affirm with them that the quiet decision to proceed in the Plan will benefit them. Give them your support by taking more time with them if they need it.

Give full explanations.

Understand that requests for more information are not so much from skepticism as from a desire to give you an intelligent "yes."

Use a quiet, calm manner.

Displaying a high level of excitement and active enthusiasm will not cause them to move toward you, because they tend to conceal their own emotions. Rather, show warmth in your eyes and in words that will reveal your steady commitment to the business.

One thing is sure, showing the Plan to a high **S** will be a process! Now that you have a general idea of their perspective, be sure to consider your own style too. If you are a High **S**, you will naturally present the Plan in a manner consistent with the preferences above. How will this relate to another **S**, a driving **D**, an influencing **I**, or a critical thinking **C**? When two or more personalities are involved, we call this a Combination. The following chart will better assist you in understanding the high **S** type in Combination with the other types.

If You are an **S**
Remember to Show Confidence in Your Presentation!

S showing...a **D**

Emphasize what they can do

Look at the power in the system

Be sure to show them results

S showing...an **I**

Emphasize their outgoing nature

Look at friends and functions

Be a little more enthusiastic

S showing...an **S**

Emphasize family benefits

Look at your success with the system

Be yourself

S showing...a **C**

Emphasize the excellent system

Look at validating materials

Be consistent and kind

SHOWING THE PLAN TO A HIGH **C** TYPE

The high **C**s may be the most careful type to which you will to Show the Plan. The **C** will want to understand completely and will question you on most every point that you make. Be encouraged, for if you can draw them to a conclusion through the experience, the **C** type will use that same conscientiousness to develop their business with you! They tend to think that building a consistent, profitable business is a reasonable idea. In Dr. Rohm's presentation, *Sponsor with Style*, he shares:

10 TECHNIQUES THAT TARGET THE **C** TYPE'S PREFERENCES WHEN SHOWING THE PLAN:

Give full explanations.

Be neat in the appearance of your circles, and do make sure your numbers are right. Work from a note card or a neat "cheat sheet" to show them that you are being careful to give them correct information.

Do not "hard sell" them.

A warm handshake is appropriate for business with a high **C**, and anything physically or emotionally closer may offend them. Validate the importance of their dreams, even though they may not appear to be very excited about them outwardly.

Provide quality answers.

Make eye contact and speak thoughtfully, so they perceive that you have actually heard them. If you really need more information for them, do not guess or generalize, but ask them if you can get a more complete answer for them.

Agree on minor points.

Make sure that you agree on major concepts, and try to be understanding about their reasoning on minor points of difference. High **C**s hate being shown that they are wrong, so agreeing on minor points builds your credibility with them.

Demonstrate patience.

You must give them permission to validate the information you give them. Be patient, and do not feel that this is a lack of confidence in you. They must have confidence in your information, and this confidence will only come when you allow them to check that information with another source.

Be conservative, not exaggerative.

If they perceive that your data is reasonable, you become trustworthy as a source of information. If you overstate statistics or predictions, they have a keen ability to focus on this. Point out the validity of the SA-4400 information as a reasonable average. Tell them that many have done more, but this is a reasonable expectation.

Provide a sincere atmosphere.

Let them know that you are confident that this business will withstand the closest examination. Give them permission in advance to carefully consider the opportunity and come to their own decision. Let them know that you want what they decide is best for them.

Explain sufficient details.

You could become sidetracked explaining how products can be shipped to Argentina, but don't try to convince them in one presentation by the abundance of your detail for every question. Provide enough basic information so that they can understand the system and that the organization has a plan that can accommodate the unexpected.

Demonstrate the value and excellence of the program.

The quality of the products, cost comparisons, and the Compensation Plan matter to high **C**s more than relationships or achieving rewards. Let them look at the Amagram and catalogs for added credibility.

Be consistent.

They will evaluate you based on your promptness, sincerity, logic, and self-control; they will evaluate the business based on its quality, ethics, and historical performance.

One thing is sure, showing the Plan to a high **C** will take a commitment! Now that you have a general idea of their perspective, be sure to consider your own style too. If you are a High **C**, you will naturally present the Plan in a manner consistent with the preferences above. How will this relate to another **C**, a driving **D**, an influencing **I**, or a supportive **S**? When two or more personalities are involved, we call this a Combination. The following chart will better assist you in understanding the high **C** type in Combination with the other types.

If You are a C
Remember to Express Your Care for Them in Your Presentation!

Emphasize goals

Look at their accomplishments

Be efficient in your use of time

C showing...a D

C showing...an I

Emphasize that you like them

Look at the people in the business

Be more willing to listen

C showing...an S

Emphasize teamwork

Look at their understanding

Be warmer and calm

C showing...a C

Emphasize excellence of the business

Look at major concepts

Be agreeable

To develop greater expertise and insight, we recommend that you:

• Order the Power Plan Pages, designed for your Franklin Planner. These special insert pages are ready reference for issues regarding your business. They include tips for showing the Plan, communicating effectively with different styles and charts for recording reminders about your Independent Business Owners.

• Order *Who Do You Think You Are Anyway?*, an in-depth reference for more complete explanations of the various personality styles in combination with one another. It will help you to understand how you can achieve harmony at work, in your family, and in your business. These products are available on the form in the back of this book.

Raising your *PQ* to Show the Plan with Style

Raising your *PQ* will make you more persuasive as you show the Plan. Persuasion is not manipulation. Manipulation means "to change by artful or unfair means so as to serve one's purpose." In contrast, Bill Gothard explains, "Persuasion is guiding vital truths around other people's mental roadblocks." You do not want to bend or break the truth. You want to share the truth in a way that another person can apply the truth to the reality of their life right now. Then they may desire to apply that truth in the near future.

An IBO had contacted a new prospect and really hoped that this prospect would expand his business into the new area where the prospect lived. One evening, he and his wife met with this prospective couple to show the Plan to them.

A smiling, excited woman warmly welcomed them into her home. She invited them into the living room, where she and her husband sat down with them. She was quick to respond as the conversation turned to dreams. While her husband quietly listened, she laughed and talked with them about her longing for a lifestyle where she was free to have fun with her kids and explore the world with her husband and children!

This IBO knew she definitely had a high *I* style! He felt her interest and appreciated her enthusiasm, but he also wanted to effectively communicate with her husband, who seemed so different. The IBO remembered that a spouse can have a style that is opposite from their partner. Looking at the *DISC* model in his Power Plan Pages, he looked opposite the high *I* to find the High *C* type. Perhaps this husband had a high *C* style!

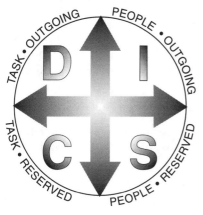

When speaking to the husband, the IBO directed the conversation to facts and figures about the business opportunity. While he seemed more interested in this, it did not seem to be the kind of information about which he really cared. He was ready to call their meeting to a close, thinking it was a waste of his time. Searching for a personal connection with this task-oriented man, the IBO noted the difference living in a large city must make in his time schedule. "Tell me," he asked the prospect, "why do you make your rush hour commute into the city every day?"

The prospect, having a high *C* style, actually hated sitting in traffic two hours a day, unable to accomplish anything meaningful! He shrugged off the question with a reserved answer: "Well, it's just part of the rat race, I guess." Then the Independent Business Owner nodded his head, smiled and replied: "Well, Will Rogers said, 'The trouble with the rat race is that, even if you win, you're still a rat!' I used to have that problem, too, until I found the way out..." Had this Independent Business Owner really found a no-nonsense way to get out of the rat race? This prospect was now willing to listen. The prospect was interested because the IBO had *DISC*overed his real need.

A tremendously profitable partnership has grown from that first meeting, because the IBO raised his *PQ* to *DISC*over his prospects' dreams and needs. In fact, those prospects became the IBO's first Emerald leg!

Raising your *PQ* is often the key to getting someone's attention and turning them around.

It is best to show the Plan by **DISC**overing the dreams of the prospects and how the business benefits them. Just as dreams are something they would really love to have *in* their lives, sometimes they may be more in touch with something they would really love to have *out* of their lives. Getting something out of their lives can at times be the major driving force that causes people to change directions in their lives. The prospect may be more strongly motivated away from something than toward something else. Here are a few examples:

Perhaps a *D* is tired of answering to leaders who won't lead. You might suggest that she really wants to be her own boss.

Maybe an *I* wants fewer constraints and more free time. You might suggest that he wants a lifestyle that is more flexible.

An *S* may be feeling used and taken for granted. You might suggest that she would like to be part of a team where each person carries her own weight.

A *C* might be frustrated by a lack of planning and constant accommodation for rushed, lower quality work. You might suggest that he would like a plan that will allow pursuit of excellence for quality goods and services.

We suggest that you always try to find the positive dreams that relate to any person's needs; keep the tone of your presentation positive! Motivation can be positive or negative, so it is important to raise your *PQ* as you carefully listen to their needs. Suggest the dreams that can meet those needs with the benefits of your business opportunity.

RAISING OUR DREAM-BUILDING *PQ*

Does your group call it "dream-building," or the "dream session," or possibly something else? Whatever you call it, it's the big "What If..." part of your presentation. Each personality style as their own dream-building patterns. The following questions would be good to ask when **DISC**overing the prospect's dream:

For the high *D*, think in terms of "What..."

What if... time and money were not an issue?

What if... you could spend the rest of your life doing the things you want to do?

What if... you could try something and knew for sure you would not fail?

What if... you could live anywhere in the world?

What if... you could own any car you wanted?

What if... you could vacation with your spouse wherever you wanted?

What if... you could take control of own your own business?

What if... you could respond with your wallet the same way your heart responds to other people's needs?

For the high *I*, think in terms of "Who..."

Who... would you like your kids going to school with?

Who... would you like your spouse spending their free time with?

Who... could help you gain financial freedom?

Who... would you like to spend your time with earning money?

Who... would you like to come to your new home?

Who... would you like to go with you on reward trips?

Who... would you like to see you when you walk across the stage?

Who... would you like to show off that dream car to?

For the *S*, think in terms of, "How..."

How... can I help you achieve your dreams?

How... can I get you the information you need to consider this opportunity?

How... can I best answer your questions?

How... can you rearrange your schedule to be able to meet with me?

How... are you feeling about where you are now in your life?

How... would you like to support your family more easily?

How... would you like to fit into your group or organization?

How... do you like to help people with the extra resources this business could generate?

For the **C**, think in terms of, Why...

Why... are you concerned about your future?

Why... is financial freedom important to you?

Why... is it important to you to be associated with a quality company?

Why... would this opportunity interest you?

Why... is this business a good plan for you?

Why... are your buying habits easy to change?

Why... do so many people like these products?

Why... would this business strengthen you and your spouse as a couple?

RIGHT WORDS, RIGHT TIME

The *right* word at the *right* time can make your presentation. How many stories have you heard from Diamonds who can laugh now, when they had cried, over the wrong word said at just the *wrong* time? There is a degree of showmanship in presenting the business Plan that all of us can learn. The legendary publisher, Joseph Pulitzer, who created the world-renowned Pulitzer Prize, penned these words as a guideline for reporters in telling a story. Remember these words as you show the Plan:

> *Put it before them briefly so they will read it,*
> *Tell them clearly so they will appreciate it,*
> *Show it picturesquely so they will remember it,*
> *And above all, accurately so they will be guided by its light.*

Joseph Pulitzer wrote this before **DISC** was developed, but can you see why his words are so powerful? Each personality type is represented in this concept:

D *Put it before them briefly so they will read it,*
I *Show it picturesquely so they will remember it,*
S *Tell them clearly so they will appreciate it,*
C *And above all, accurately so they will be guided by its light.*

Choose words that will address each personality type as you raise your **PQ** to communicate with their style. Your presentation will be more persuasive if it is personal. Your excitement will show as you share your wonderful experiences in the business. Remember that *you* are the part of your organization that *they* can see! A useful technique to lower resistance is the "feel, felt, found" method. It can be a bridge from your experience to a quality answer to their question.

The Feel, Felt, Found Method

I know how you feel means I identify with you.

In fact, I felt the same way means I understand; I was there, too.

May I tell you what I found? means what I found may help you, too.

Features and Benefits

The last focus as you formulate your questions and statements for Showing the Plan with Style is learning to sell benefits instead of features. *Hold onto your hat*! This is one of Dr. Rohm's favorite parts of the book! As we worked on this material, it helped him to better see the difference between *what any product has* versus *why people actually need it*!

We naturally seem to want to explain all the features of the business, but we may never connect those features with the benefits that they provide. Benefits, not features, meet the needs of the prospect. Stewart will never forget the experience that taught him the difference between a feature and a benefit, as he explains:

> *As a college student struggling to pay my bills, I decided to sell insurance for a small Independent Insurance Agency. The regional representative for a large life insurance company came to the office*

for my training. I was only twenty-one; he was soon to retire from a long career of selling life insurance. We sat at my small desk, empty except for a phone for prospecting calls.

He pulled a pen from his pocket and said, "Sell me this pen." I gave him a puzzled look, to which he repeated, "Sell me this pen." I confidently stated, "I am not trying to sell pens. I am trying to sell life insurance!" He firmly responded, "If you can't sell me this pen, you can't sell someone life insurance." I took the hint and picked up the pen. I described the pen carefully. "Sir, this pen writes in black ink. It has a silver clip. It has a cap to cover the tip. It is not a very expensive pen. You should buy this pen!" I thought I had done a great job!

The old salesman took the pen from me and said, "Let me sell you this pen." He began by asking me why I might need a pen. I needed a pen to write letters, take notes, and fill out insurance application forms, I told him. "Stewart, you shared with me that you need a pen to be able to do your work. This pen uses black ink, which is important to you because most insurance applications must be filled out in black. The black ink is also easier for a copy machine to make good copies from, and you need copies of your applications. This silver clip is made from a lightweight material that isn't very heavy in your pocket. The clip keeps the pen in your pocket so that you won't lose it. A salesman must have a pen to complete an application! The cap will keep the pen from drying out so that it will last a long time. Finally, the cost of this pen is low, so that you will spend less money for this pen than you might for another. How many pens would you like to buy?"

Stewart had tried to sell the master salesman by explaining all the features of the pen. The master salesman sold Stewart by explaining how each feature would benefit Stewart. What a fantastic difference! Notice how the experienced salesman related features to benefits:

Feature: The pen has black ink.
Benefits: Legal forms require black ink. Black ink makes better copies.
Feature: The pen has a lightweight silver clip.
Benefit: This looks professional for a good impression. It keeps the pen in your pocket to prevent losing it.
Feature: The pen has a removable cap.
Benefit: This keeps the pen from drying out so it will work.
Feature: This pen is economical.
Benefit: This pen will save you money.

The feature is what the product does, and the benefit is what it will do for the customer!

Powerful IDEA

In any kind of selling, experience demonstrates that people buy benefits, not features. Have you ever seen a McDonald's commercial on television? They always sell you the benefit of how wonderful a trip to their restaurant will be. They never focus on the feature of their food. That is incidental. Getting you in the restaurant is what they want to do!

A Feature is:
A characteristic
A peculiarity
A distinctive part
Structure, form or appearance

A Benefit is:
Something that promotes well being
Something that is good for a person
An advantage
Something that brings personal gain

In showing the Plan, ask yourself:
What benefit does this feature offer to each type?

Look at this example:

Feature: E-commerce product order placement

Benefit to the High *D*:

Fast, direct order placement for speedy delivery

Benefit to the High *I*:

Seeing so many exciting products quickly, in living color

Benefit to the High *S*:

Ability to shop without pressure from a salesperson

Benefit to the High *C*:

Competitive products and pricing available for their evaluation

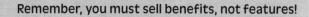

Powerful IDEA   Remember, you must sell benefits, not features!

Showing the Plan with Style takes practice. As you understand yourself, understand your prospect and adapt your presentation to their style, you will be increasingly effective in your presentation. Finding the right questions and using the right words to sell benefits to your prospect will empower you to persuade them. You can Show the Plan with Style!

A TAKE ACTION

CHAPTER TWELVE

PERSONAL ACTION PLAN

Question 1: Pick one of the *DISC* styles different from your own. Write down three ways that you can adapt your presentation of the plan for a person with that high style.

My Style_____Their Style_____ 3 ways I can adapt:

1. _____

2. _____

3. _____

Question 2: Thinking about one of your favorite products, describe its **benefits** (not features) to each *DISC* type.

Product Name _____

Benefits to each type:

D _____

I _____

S _____

C _____

Follow Through with Style

Before you contact, invite and show the Plan with style, you are able to plan your interaction with your prospect in many ways. You can make the initial contact, then think about the other person's style before you invite him or her. You can plan and present your invitation according to their style. Before you show the Plan, you can carefully list your open probes and statements of benefits to appeal to their personality style. The next stage, as you follow up, will usually be more complex and responsive. During the follow up process there will be many phone calls, questions answered, objections met, and time allowed for your prospect to reach a decision. We would like to call this *follow through with style*, because this is where the real relationship building begins, and how you raise your *Personality Quotient* will show in how you follow through to a great start! You will begin to get to know your prospect personally, and will begin to *DISC*over many of their strengths and struggles. You will have the opportunity to begin a good relationship as you respond to them with understanding and acceptance. It is this relationship, more than anything else, which will attract them to the business and keep them building it with you.

In chapter two, we called this Relationship Marketing and discussed how very important it is in this business. Your prospect will begin to see if you really are who you say you are. Your prospect will see your real excitement in the business, your dreams, your understanding of their dreams, and your desire to meet their needs. As you follow through, the real questions are answered, objections are addressed, and decisions are made. Your success will depend greatly upon your *PQ* as you follow through with style.

We will discuss this success in our upcoming book, *The Facets of Life*, empowering you to understand how you can *DISC*over fulfillment in all aspects of life. Look for it!

While your follow through with any prospect will be more personal, complex and responsive, we can anticipate how personality styles affect the kinds of questions that are asked and their desired answers. We will explore personality insights on objections and how to best respond to them. We will **DISC**over how the different styles make decisions and how to help their decision-making process. We will learn to recognize the right time to *Simply Ask* them to join you in the business.

 Follow up is really follow through! The successful IBO will consistently follow through by answering questions, meeting objections, enhancing decisions, and building relationships.

*PQ*ING YOUR PROSPECT'S ATTITUDES

Most of the things we do each day, we do by habit. A habit starts with a decision, and is repeated until it is expected and comfortable for the person. Making a different decision requires effort, and changing a habit requires more effort. When you show the Plan to someone, you are suggesting that they change buying habits and make decisions about products. You are asking them to decide to do something new, to build a business. When they react with skepticism, objections or indifference, they do not necessarily mean "no," they may just mean "not yet." You may not yet have given them reasons that are compelling enough for them to make a decision. They are responding to what you have given them, and are expressing their opinion of it.

Skepticism and Objections

When your prospect expresses skepticism or raises objections, recognize that this is good! Why? You know that:

> The prospect is thinking and listening to you.
>
> You have **DISC**overed a need.
>
> You have an opportunity to **DISC**over a benefit that may compel them to reach a decision.
>
> Your persuasion, as you offer more information, can give them the compelling reasons they need to decide.

The prospect is usually seeking more facts. What they really need is to understand that these facts have benefits that will give them compelling reasons to reach a decision. They will retain or reform their opinion based on these compelling reasons. Compelling reasons must be based on their needs and dreams.

Indifference

When your prospect expresses indifference, you may feel that this is a less threatening rejection than objections. Indifference can be a more difficult attitude to deal with, however, because it means that you have not yet found benefits that interest them. You know that:

> You need to probe again to **DISC**over their needs.

> You must offer them the benefits that can meet their needs.

> You must show compelling reasons for them to reach a decision.

Attitudes expressed are simply signposts. They give you direction to areas where you need to offer explanations as compelling reasons for a positive decision. Have you ever tried to find a house by a signpost that has been turned? How frustrating it is to go down a street that is clearly marked, but as you explore further, you find that the sign has been turned. You have correctly read the signpost but gone down the wrong street! You had good intentions, but you were following the wrong directions. Sometimes expressed attitudes are like a turned signpost, directing you to the wrong objection. For example, your prospect may say, "I am not interested." Talk with them and try to **DISC**over their needs. You may find that the underlying objection is "I just got chewed out for signing up for something else that my spouse didn't like, and I do not want that to happen again!" This is a very different signpost, isn't it? How would you meet this objection?

Address the attitude – the objection, skepticism or indifference. Raise your **PQ** to find compelling reasons for them to make a positive decision!

WELCOME QUESTIONS AND OBJECTIONS AS YOUR BEST FRIEND

Stewart remembers learning very early in his business career that questions and objections are not rejection to be avoided at all costs. He saw that as long as his prospect was asking questions and raising objections, he was learning more about the prospect's thinking. He then could understand what he needed to say or do to find compelling reasons for the person to buy his product. A prospect's questions and objections are your opportunity to achieve success. As a prospect questions and raises objections, you are learning about them. You are one step closer to asking them to join your organization.

As your prospect raises an objection and you respond, you will interact in *Combination*. A Combination occurs whenever two personality styles interact. If you are talking with a prospect couple, the Combination is more complex, involving the interaction between you and the husband, you and the wife, and between the husband and the wife. If your husband or wife is also involved in the conversation, the interactions multiply again! It is vital that you raise your *PQ* to understand the dynamics that are occurring.

*DISC*OVERING QUESTIONS AND OBJECTIONS

Each *DISC* personality type raises questions and objections differently. Different types will express different attitudes, so they will choose different words too. Sometimes you will need to ask them questions to enable you to understand the reasoning behind their questions or objections. Because this is in Combination with your personality style, remember to raise your *PQ* and seek understanding with them!

The High *D* naturally exercises power to solve problems. They will ask questions or raise objections in ways that makes you feel like they are attacking you. Remember that they are really just naturally attacking the problem, not you! What they want you to tell them is that you really believe what you are saying. They want you to give them choices so that they feel that they can solve the problem through their decision. If the high **D** seems indifferent to your presentation, ask them what would attract their interest, and offer choices to generate response if necessary. Power is the high **D**'s priority.

The High **I** will ask questions or raise objections in a fun and interesting way. They may make a joke that is hard for you to recognize as an objection, because they do not want to feel your rejection. They will respond well if you focus on them. Let them know that you like them enough to want their approval of what you have shared. Tell them a short story and ask if they have had a similar experience. The high **I** may respond with indifference when they *do* have an objection, so make sure to engage them in casual conversation in order to draw out their response. Real indifference from a high **I** probably means that you may need to introduce them to more people in the business. People are the high **I**s priority.

The High **S** will ask questions or raise objections in a softer and more timid manner. They will probably apologize for any question they ask. They will need your affirmation, so be sure to tell them how glad you are that they did ask. Offer them a friendly explanation, and be sure to give them time to think about it. Tell them that after they have had time to think about it, you would appreciate their response. Ask them if you can talk again at a later time. Pace is the high **S**s priority.

The High **C** will ask many questions concerning their objections. They will require detailed answers and your permission to validate the information that you have given them. They will not be satisfied until they have received complete answers and have taken your information to another source for validation. The other source may be someone who they feel is knowledgeable in that field, or supporting data from a different source. Remember, the high **C** will not make a decision based solely on what you say, no matter how convincing it is. The best way to increase your credibility with them is to tell them that you know that they will want to think about what you have told them and encourage them to check out your information. Procedure is the high **C**s priority.

*DISC*OVERING RESPONSES TO QUESTIONS AND OBJECTIONS

Each *DISC* personality type responds to questions and objections differently. Different types have different attitudes about questions and objections, so they will use different words too. Sometimes you will need to adapt your style to answer in a way that they will understand. Because this is in Combination with your personality style, remember to raise your *PQ* and seek understanding with them!

The High *D* will naturally exercise power in giving quick answers that are intended to solve problems immediately. They will need to recognize that the prospect needs the opportunity to think about what they have said and to reach their own decision. When the High *D* has offered a response, they must also be careful to give the prospect permission to ask another question. The High *D* must raise their *PQ* to remember that a compelling reason for another type has more to do with people (*I*), pace (*S*) or procedure (*C*), than power (*D*).

The High *I* will naturally talk to persuade you that their answer is more fun, and that their answer will be acceptable to everyone. They will need to recognize that the prospect needs more information than they might naturally give, and wants the opportunity to think about what they have said and to reach their own decision. When the High *I* has offered a response, they must also be careful to give the prospect permission to ask for more detailed information. The High *I* must raise their *PQ* to remember that a compelling reason for another type has more to do with power (*D*), pace (*S*) or procedure (*C*), than people (*I*).

The High *S* will naturally keep a slower pace, and will hesitate to answer objections because they want predictability. They want to feel comfortable that they can stick to routine and give proven answers from their upline. They will need to recognize that the prospect appreciates the opportunity to receive their answers, so that the prospect can think about it and reach their own decision. When the High *S* has offered a response, they must also be confident, giving the prospect the opportunity to make a decision. The High *S* must raise their **PQ** to remember that a compelling reason for another type has more to do with power (**D**), people (**I**) or procedure (**C**), than pace (**S**).

The High **C** will naturally deal with facts and follow procedure carefully as they answer objections. They will need to recognize that the prospect needs to know how they feel about the opportunity for the prospect to reach their own decision. When the High **C** offers a response, they must be careful to give the prospect permission to express their own feelings and to ask another question. The High **C** must raise their **PQ** to remember that a compelling reason for another type has more to do with power (**D**), people (**I**) or pace (**S**), than procedure (**C**).

NOT AGAINST YOU, BUT FOR THEMSELVES!

Dr. Rohm loves to say, "People don't do things *against* you. They do things *for* themselves!" Always treat your prospect as if you know this! Be confident that they are only trying to understand so that they can decide if this business is for them. This means that both you and your prospect are working toward the very same objective! You want to determine if your prospect would work hard, and really be good in this business. You want them to decide if they could become a positive, contributing member of your team. Your prospect wants to determine if they can work with you. They want to decide if this business would bring them success. Your objectives and the objectives of your prospect are like the two sides of a coin. You cannot have one without the other!

As you understand the meaning of an objection, they will usually fall into two major categories:

> 1. Misunderstandings about your business plan and products, caused by a lack of information.

> 2. Drawbacks that exist, in your business plan or in the products, which you are unable to directly satisfy. These drawbacks lead to the prospect's dislike of, or dissatisfaction with, your business.

You can handle an objection due to a misunderstanding once you have a clear understanding of the reason for the objection.

You should:

Ask an open probe to confirm the prospect's need.

Offer supporting statements to clear up misunderstandings.

When a prospect raises an objection because of something that they misunderstood, they are actually providing you with useful, although negative, information about their needs. The first step in handling a misunderstanding is to probe to confirm the prospect's need. Doing so helps you focus on the prospect's desire or need, instead of focusing on the opposition to your business opportunity.

Remember that you can always regain control by asking an open probe question.

HARMONIZING OBJECTIONS

Responding to objections in a way that creates harmony requires effort. You need to make the effort to raise your **PQ**. This means that you keep in mind your own personality style in combination with your prospect's style. You listen to their objections and seek to understand the basis for their objection. You adapt your style so that you respond to them in a way that answers their objection in words that they will understand. By making eye contact, being friendly and respectful, you communicate your sincere interest in them and in their decision.

Most people who are really looking for financial options want compelling reasons to say *yes*—but their compelling reasons may not be the same as yours would be. They want to know that your solution has met your needs and they want to understand how it can meet theirs, too. Their questions and objections are simply a request for more information. Get to know them so that you can provide the information they need, in a way that appeals to their personality style.

This business, like any business, has certain objections that are peculiar to it. We suggest that you sit down with your upline to write down the objections and responses that are common in your organization's business. As you show the Plan, take notes on the objections that you have trouble handling. Share this information with your upline and ask for their coaching.

Here are some common objections that may come up in your discussion. We want you to see how personality styles relate to objections.

High *D* type objection: "I am in a meeting—I can't talk now!"

Response: "I do not want to interrupt you. When may I call you back?"

High *I* type objection: "Everything is going great for me right now! I don't need to worry about a new business."

Response: "I am glad things are great for you right now! I'd like to introduce you to some successfull business people who would enjoy meeting you!"

High *S* type objection: "My spouse really needs to be involved in this decision."

Response: "I am so glad that you want your spouse to be involved. When will he/she be available? When would be a good time to call back to arrange to meet with both of you?"

High *C* type objection: "I am afraid I am just not interested."

Response: "I can relate to that. I was not interested at first, until I understood how this business could substantially increase my income. What would you think about spending just one hour to look at some facts and figures?"

Sit down with your upline and make a list of objections and responses. Your preparation will really increase your confidence and success.

MAKING DECISIONS

Each personality style naturally approaches decisions differently. You know some people who are very impulsive in decision-making; you know others who feel stressed if they must make any decision quickly. Understanding your prospect's decision-making style, based on their basic priority, can help you pace your follow-through process.

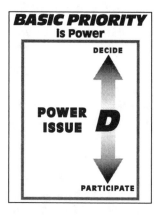

This **Basic Priority** picture shows that the higher from the midline that the **D** plotting point lies, the greater the intensity of the **D** type in the person's style. The higher the intensity of the **D** type, the higher their priority for using **Power** to **decide** in order *to solve problems*. They show little in the way of self-doubt. They prefer to be in control, and if given the option, they will happily decide for themselves and everyone else!

On the other side of the **D** Priority, the lower from the midline that the **D** plotting point lies, the stronger will be their priority in the opposite direction. The way they exercise **Power** is to **participate** in reaching a decision with a consensus of opinion from everyone involved. They prefer *to be a team player*, and if given the option, they will just participate in the process. In the end, they will use power as they participate, but allow the group to decide.

This **Basic Priority** picture shows that the higher from the midline that the **I** plotting point lies, the greater the intensity of the **I** type in the person's style. The higher the intensity of the **I** type, the higher their priority is in approaching **People** to **interact** in order *to persuade others*. They will often make impulsive decisions based on others' approval of what they have said. They prefer to think out loud, and if given the option, they will make the popular decision!

On the other side of the *I* Priority, the lower from the midline that the *I* plotting point lies, the stronger will be their priority in the opposite direction. They prefer to distance themselves from **People** and to **isolate** themselves from a given situation. They often prefer to isolate themselves by dealing with just one person at a time. The low *I* type reaches a decision logically, by isolating themselves to observe a situation and listen to many viewpoints. They prefer *to be persuaded*, and if given the option, they will decide logically based on their isolated observation.

The *motor* of both of these outgoing high *D* and high *I* types runs fast! They are "go and do" types. In the fable of *The Tortoise and the Hare*, they are the hare. You should not plan to hold their attention very long. In your interactions with them, use your time wisely. You know the high *D*s schedule will be tight, and you do not want them to fear that every time you get together, it will turn into an endless marathon. With the high *I*, you must take the time to be friendly, but you may lose their interest at their impulse, so make the most of their attention! You could chat your way through the appointment and never get down to business. Remember, for both of these fast-paced styles, their high energy will challenge you. Just channel that energy in the right direction for your business!

This **Basic Priority** picture shows that the higher from the midline that the *S* plotting point lies, the greater the intensity of the *S* type in the person's style. The higher the intensity of the *S* type, the higher their priority is for **Predictability** through **routine** in an unchanging, stable environment. They like sticking with what works. They prefer *to maintain the status quo*, and if pushed too hard or too quickly, they will stubbornly, quietly resist change!

BASIC PRIORITY
is Predictability

ROUTINE

PREDICT-
ABILITY
ISSUE *S*

CHANGE

On the other side of the *S* Priority, the lower from the midline that the *S* plotting point lies, the stronger will be their priority for change. Routine is boring to them, so they prefer to see **Predictability** as an opportunity to **change** their environment. They prefer *to be spontaneous*, and if given the option, they will decide to try something different.

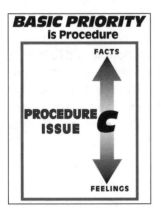

BASIC PRIORITY
is Procedure

FACTS

PROCEDURE
ISSUE **C**

FEELINGS

This **Basic Priority** picture shows that the higher from the midline that the **C** plotting point lies, the greater the intensity of the **C** type in the person's style. The higher the intensity of the **C** type, the more comfortable the person is in using **Procedure** according to **Facts** in an environment with a well-defined structure. They want lots of facts and information in defined order. Things must be organized so that everyone plays by the rules! They prefer *to uphold principles*, and if given the option, they will objectively decide on the correct procedure!

On the other side of the **C** Priority, the lower from the midline that the **C** plotting point lies, the less comfortable they tend to be in a rigid structure with strict rules. They prefer to use **Procedure** according to their **Feelings** in an environment where they are free and independent. They prefer *self-expression*, and if something touches their feelings, they will decide instinctively and subjectively, according to those feelings.

In both of these high **S** and high **C** types, the *motor* is idling more slowly, reserving their power rather than racing fast. They are more likely to "sit and think" than to "go and do." In the fable *The Tortoise and the Hare*, they are the tortoise. In your interactions with them, pace yourself more slowly. They can be very effective, and their reserved energy will produce results through a process. Respect the time they have to meet with you. Be punctual, use your time to answer their appropriate questions and then give them time to respond back to you.

THINKER

At Personality Insights, we know that if you give an **S** or a **C** time to think about the business opportunity, you probably will come back to *close* the deal. If you give a **D** or an **I** time to think about it, you probably will come back to *lose* the deal!

Here is a real-life example from the world of automobile sales:

A successful Pontiac salesman, who has a high **S** style, showed a new vehicle to a couple. Because he understood **DISC** personality types, he identified both the husband and wife as having high **C** styles. The couple told him that they planned to buy a Ford, but they had come to his dealership simply to pick up some information on a comparable Pontiac model. He understood that both the husband and wife would proceed to buy the Ford after they had information from him to validate their purchase of the Ford.

He understood their need to validate information meant that his expressive excitement about his car would not help him make the sale. He did not push them in any way, but carefully supplied them the variety of information they had requested. Knowing that they were on their way to the nearby Ford dealership, he recommended to them a particular Ford salesman. He knew the salesman had a high **D** style, but also that this Ford salesman knew nothing about **DISC**!

Why did he recommend a salesman who knew nothing about **DISC**? The Pontiac salesman expected that the high **D** Ford salesman would naturally try to push the couple to decide. The Pontiac salesman hoped that they would then come back to him and buy the Pontiac. Predictably, the high **D** salesman tried to pressure them to close the sale immediately. The couple resisted his efforts and left. After a few days of gathering even more information, they returned to the Pontiac dealership and bought the Pontiac from the friendly salesman.

Did the Pontiac salesman unfairly manipulate that couple? Not at all! He effectively influenced their decision by understanding their personality style decision-making priority. Whether we like it or not, people buy from people they like! If you remember that *people do things for themselves, not against you*, you will understand that they like to buy from you when you meet their needs! The Pontiac salesman met their need for facts by giving them information. He also satisfied their priority for procedure by giving them permission and the time to validate that information with another source. He satisfied their priority and met their needs, so they decided to buy from him!

HELPING THEM ALONG

In a follow-through meeting, establish a positive atmosphere. Compliment your prospects about something that you genuinely appreciate. Flattery is insincere, and most people will feel that insincerity. Greet them warmly and let them know that you are glad to be with them again. If you can sit at the kitchen table again, all the better. Light conversation, about something that interests both of you, can put your prospects at ease. If they offer you something to drink, accept it with thanks. Allow them to serve you, even if you are not thirsty. Your interaction with them is a bridge to building a relationship with them.

Let them know that you value them, because you have been thinking of them. Demonstrate your belief in them by bringing them a piece of literature that relates to their dream—a travel brochure, a pamphlet about a car, a homebuilder's layout. It communicates that you listened to them, you have thought about them, and that you value what is important to them. This literature will springboard you back into their dreams. Do not ask, "Do you really want to do this?" Instead, direct the conversation to the steps that will bring their first goals within reach. Follow their dream from entering the business to realizing their dream.

Your upline has a specific pattern for follow-through meetings, so we do not want to change that pattern. Do keep in mind that you want your prospect to say "yes" often during this process. This is the place for the closed probe, a question that you know will render a "yes" response. You can ask certain questions and make comments that elicit a "yes" response. They may help your prospects feel more comfortable with you because you are in agreement with each other on issues that are important to them.

People will feel that you truly understand them and what is important in their lives when your statements identify their wants and needs, their likes and dislikes. According to research by Ron Ball, money ranks only at *Number Five* on a list of *What is Really Important*. Ron says, "People are starving for a sense of importance and recognition."

 To understand the importance of security and the significance of recognition, be sure to look for our new book, *The Facets of Life*, soon to be published!

Recognize Buying Signals

Closing is a request to receive a positive response for a specific action. It requires sensitive timing. Perfect timing for closing comes when the prospect gives "buying signals," so being familiar with them is necessary for an effective close.

Buying signals are the way the prospect shows you that they are ready to act, or at least to react favorably to what you are saying. You should start the closing process when you begin receiving these signals. Failing to close at the appropriate time may cause you to talk yourself out of a sale.

Examples of buying signals include:

1. Specific statements of agreement about benefits or needs. "Yes, this could really help us financially."

2. Questions about what is involved in signing up, how long it takes to go direct, what levels of achievement mean, how easy is it to begin the monthly delivery system, or other specifics.

3. Questions about price. If someone did not feel that they could use what you are offering, they would not care about the price. When a price question arises, they feel that what you are offering has value. Their questions about price relate to how high they perceive that value to be, compared to the price. Expect a **C** to ask about price.

These are typical buying signals; the actual wording will vary according to personality types. Outgoing styles will be quick to give buying signals, while reserved styles will be more hesitant. Be thoroughly familiar with the buying signals you may encounter in your presentation situations. Ask your upline to share their experiences with buying signals. When the signals appear, ask a closed probe question to begin closing. If the prospect is not yet ready to sign up, they will indicate that by asking additional questions or raising objections.

When you recognize a buying signal, you should use your prepared closed probe question to test the prospect's reaction. Their agreement may be expressed in words or it may be reflected in their tone of voice or manner. When you sense a favorable reaction, either from diminished resistance or from signs of interest, begin to close. Close when the pace slows down in the conversation, when they are speaking in favor of your opportunity, or when they start asking questions related to signing up or getting started in the business.

The close represents one of the most difficult sales techniques. You have adapted your style to answer questions and meet objections as you offer benefits to satisfy needs. When you have arrived at a point where there is mutual agreement, you must now make it easy for them to make the decision to sign up with your organization.

SIMPLY ASK

Numerous studies explore the motivational forces that create a sale. The studies listed thousands of reasons why the customer was motivated to buy and they included everything from profit potential to the color of the salesperson's eyes. But in 97 out of 100 cases, the customers had to be *asked to buy* before the salesperson could close the sale. Zig Ziglar says this is the number one reason why people do not buy!

If you were to ask any one of Stewart's children what this means, they would tell you emphatically "You don't get anything until you ask for it!" Everyday, in this busy, demanding world, all of us are being asked to do this, do that, come here, go there, say this, or don't say that. So many demands! Unless we are asked to do something, most of us never will. How many times have you subconsciously waited for the salesperson to ask you to buy their product? The next time you are dealing with a salesperson, think about how long it takes them to ask for the order and how long you are willing to wait until they do. Each personality style must ask for the order. They must *simply ask* someone to join their organization. Understanding how the different styles will ask and respond is essential to a successful close.

The high **D** type will deliver a powerful close. They will simply ask a direct question, and want an immediate, firm response. They may need to guard their **PQ** to be less forceful as they close.

The high **I** type will deliver a popular close. They will want you to like them enough to sign up, so they may be very sensitive to the prospect's feelings before they simply ask. They may need to listen more as they close.

The high **S** type will be slow to close. They will want a prospect's affirmation long before they will simply ask. They may need to be more confident as they close.

The high **C** type will be cautious as they close. They may try to provide every fact to answer every possible question before they will simply ask. They may need to learn to recognize the feelings of the other person as they begin to close effectively.

You may understand your personality style. You may understand the style of your prospect. You may adapt your follow through to answer their questions, meet their objections, and satisfy their needs. At this point, you may *simply ask* them to become part of your organization. Even when you have done all this as well as you know how, the answer still may be *no*. What do you do? You realize that you have done all of these things and think about what you have learned in the process. You recognize that your prospect may simply not be ready to say *yes*. You appreciate the fact that you have been successful in completing this process. You try again. The next time, the prospect may say *Yes*! That will happen, and when it does, the next chapter will illustrate how you can guide them into "Getting Started with Style!"

A TAKE ACTION

CHAPTER THIRTEEN

PERSONAL ACTION PLAN

Question 1: As you learn to follow through with style, list a primary objection you have faced from each of the **DISC** styles, and how you *now* would answer each objection for them:

D type

Objection:

Answer: _____

I type

Objection:

Answer: _____

S type

Objection:

Answer: _____

C type

Objection:

Answer: _____

Question 2: In thinking about the information about buying signals, list two ideas from the chapter that you will now begin to recognize as signals to begin closing: _____

_____

Getting Started with Style!

Fail to plan, and you plan to fail. This vital truth is so important! You must have a good plan before you begin a business: know what you plan to do, how you plan to do it, and why the steps in your plan are important. Management expert Peter Drucker adds one more essential element: *"Plans are only good intentions unless they immediately degenerate into hard work."*

This second vital truth is that *you must do the work!* We worked with a Diamond who had been introduced years ago to personality temperaments using the old Greek terms. We all laughed and nodded in agreement when he told an audience of IBOs: "You might be a Sanguine or a Choleric or a Buick LeSabre—but you're still gonna do the things Diamonds do if you want to be a Diamond!" Ask any Diamond, and they will tell you that they did not become a Diamond by talking, wishing, or planning. Please don't think that understanding **DISC** is going to replace your hard work; it should simply make your hard work more productive.

Jay Van Andel says it this way:

> *Years ago, we decided we had to act—to work— whatever the conditions were at any given time. If we had waited for the "right time" to launch Amway, if we had waited and waited for some "magic moment" to materialize, there may never have been an Amway at all.*

Because you know today's difficulties but you have yet to know tomorrow's, you always know some reason why tomorrow would be a better time than today. Rich DeVos once said, "Remember that the easiest thing to find in God's green earth is someone to tell you all the things you cannot do." Does it really make a difference if you are hearing, "You *can't* do it!" from friends, or relatives, or people at work or church, or from the doubtful little voice inside? You have today! You have no guarantee of tomorrow! You *can* develop your business, and *today* may be the best day to start!

Do you think you don't have enough money to invest in business support materials? Or do you feel that your schedule doesn't permit you to show the Plan? Or do you worry because you have not memorized everything in the Plan? You will have a better chance of success by doing something, rather than doing nothing. If you do not have much time to put in, improve what you put into the time! All business operates under this rule. Lee Iacocca wrote:

> *So what do we do? Anything. Something. So long as we don't just sit there. If we screw up, start over. Try something else. If we wait until we've satisfied all the uncertainties, it may be too late.*

In 1962, a new singing group recorded its first album. They were not well known, except in Liverpool, England. Studio time was expensive and schedules were full, so EMI Records budgeted only one day of studio recording time to complete all ten new songs. They decided to work with what they had. Recorded in just ten hours, that album would spend more than six months at the top of the charts. It began one of the most amazing careers in music history. If they had waited for a better time, we might never have known them as the Beatles!

Rich DeVos wrote, "One never knows what he might accomplish until he tries. That is so simple that some people completely overlook it." You will be more comfortable as you practice and learn the business. We think, because things are difficult, that we do not dare to try. It is because we do not dare to try, that things are difficult! What can we do? Let's get started!

*PQ*ING YOUR PLAN

Getting off to a good start means growing in the business. You need a plan, and your upline can provide the information, experience, and support you need for your plan. This chapter will help you to *PQ* your plan and increase your effectiveness.

Would you be surprised that every personality type looks differently at starting their business? Remember the story of the new IBO buying a necktie? Just as different styles will use a different approach to buying a necktie, different styles will plan and build their business using a different approach. One type may be very effective in one part, while another type may be comfortable at another stage. We can learn something from each type for an effective plan.

In Chapter Three we began to explore the concept of your *Personality Quotient*. We can use these four steps in raising your *PQ* as you are getting started in the business:

 Step 1. *Understanding yourself* as the upline, and how your style will naturally approach coaching someone in getting started.

 Step 2. *Understanding another person* as a new IBO and how their style will naturally approach getting started.

 Step 3. *Adapting your style to have a better relationship* with your new IBO.

Step 4. *Building better teams* both upline and downline, where *T*ogether *E*veryone *A*chieves *M*ore!

Styles and *PQ*

As your understanding of *DISC* has grown, you understand more about your style. Your style has one predominant type, the highest type in your style. The traits of that *DISC* type will *most often* describe you. You may also have one or two other high types in your style, and if you do, you will find that the traits of the other high types in your style *may often* describe you. This is how we understand our personality style blend. It is important to remember that no one person is a true type, having all the behavior traits of one *DISC* type. Your style is a unique blend, and the style of any other person is also a unique blend. *DISC* helps us see that people with a similar style will behave in a similar way under similar circumstances. Raising your *PQ* means growing in your understanding, not putting people in boxes. In this chapter, your understanding will grow and extend to actually learning how to *build better teams where T*ogether *E*veryone *A*chieves *M*ore! Getting started with style involves each of the four *PQ* steps as they relate to each personality type.

The high **D** type is a task-oriented, outgoing individual. Let's look at how the high **D** type approaches getting started in the business.

 Step 1. *Understanding yourself* as the upline, and how your style will naturally approach coaching someone in getting started.

Now that you have been successful in sponsoring a new IBO, if you have a high **D** style, you will naturally want to take control and make things happen. The high **D** type is driving and determined, and will be quick to get out and bring new people into their group. You will have quick answers to provide the new IBO with the information they need to start bringing people into the business themselves. These high **D** type strengths can serve you well. Out of control, however, these same strengths can become areas of struggle that can hinder your success. You will need to understand the importance of applying the system that your organization is presently using. The high **D** type will naturally want to design their own system, before fully understanding and applying the proven system of your organization. Slow down and use the system of your organization already in place, before trying to make your own system. You will find that it will pay off with big success.

 Step 2. *Understanding another* person as a new IBO and how their style will naturally approach getting started.

If your new IBO has a high **D** style, they will naturally want to take control, make things happen and do it their way. They will be very direct and get results. In your coaching, you will need to be prepared to give them the system core materials right away, and offer them the information, answers, reasons, and business support materials that will empower a high **D** style to get results. Several IBOs have told us that they make a list of the most common bottom line questions a high **D** type would ask, along with the specific answers. This will empower their driving style. Be a confident leader, and they will work hard to produce great results!

Step 3. *Adapting your style to have a better relationship* with your new IBO.

As a high **D** style, you will quickly develop a plan to be successful. You will get started quickly and easily, and expect your new IBO to do the same. If your new IBO has a different style, you may be really frustrated if they talk a lot, but do little; or hesitate to do anything at all; or want to study the system to death! Since only about ten percent of the population are high **D** types, you will need some of the other styles in your group! Try to be patient with them, for you will find that their strength in other parts of building your team will make you more successful in building a strong business. Work with them according to their styles to help them get started. Coach them by showing the Plan with them and encouraging their efforts. Your example, along with developing an attitude of teamwork, will be the start of a better relationship with your new IBO.

Step 4. *Building better teams both upline and downline, where **T**ogether **E**veryone **A**chieves **M**ore!*

As a high **D** style, you will be quick to ask someone to join your team. You may also be quick to *offend* an IBO who has a different style, because you think that your style looks better as you begin together. If you understand that you will achieve more by keeping them on your team, you will have taken an important step as a high **D** style in building a better team. Make it clear that you understand you are not their "boss", but do give them assignments to read books and listen to tapes, and to write down their questions or ideas. Simply ask them to commit to doing this, and then you must commit to discussing it with them. Let them take responsibility for their part in building their business, and be sure to be there to coach whenever they ask.

The high *I* type is a people-oriented, outgoing individual. Let's look at how the high *I* type approaches getting started in the business.

Step 1. *Understanding yourself* as the upline, and how your style will naturally approach coaching someone in getting started.

Now that you have been successful in sponsoring a new IBO, your high *I* style will naturally be excited about it! The high *I* type is enthusiastic and fun-loving, and will be quick to talk to people about coming into their group. You will enjoy getting together with the new IBO and will be optimistic and communicative as you start bringing people into the business. These high *I* type strengths can serve you well. Out of control, however, these same strengths can become areas of struggle that can hinder your success. You will need to remember the importance of applying the system that your organization is presently using. The high *I* type will naturally want to get involved with the organization, but may be directionless in working the proven system of your organization. Enjoy your friendly conversations, but find an attention grabber that will lead you to share your important business story and the system used in your organization. You will find that it will pay off with big success.

Step 2. *Understanding another person* as a new IBO and how their style will naturally approach getting started.

If your new IBO has a high *I* style, they will naturally want to have fun and talk with you! They will be very excited and talkative. In your coaching, you will need to be prepared to give them friendly direction to the system by putting core materials in their hands right away! Because they do better with short-term projects, talk enthusiastically with them about the information, answers, reasons, and business support materials that will empower a high *I* type to get immediate results. Several IBOs have told us that they like to do the paperwork with a high *I* style, or to depend on the IBO's spouse who has another style. This will empower their inspiring style. Be an enthusiastic leader, and they will work hard to produce great results!

 Step 3. *Adapting your style to have a better relationship* with your new IBO.

As a high *I* style, you will talk to many people to be successful. You will meet new prospects quickly and easily, and expect your new IBO to do the same. If your new IBO has a different style, you may be really frustrated if they demand bottom-line answers; or hesitate to do anything at all; or want to study the system to death! Since high *I* types love to have so many people, you will need some of the other styles in your group! Try to be focused with them, for you will find that their strength in other parts of building your team will make you more successful in building a strong business. Work with them according to their styles to help them get started. Coach them by showing the Plan with them and encouraging their efforts. Your example, along with developing an attitude of teamwork, will be the start of a better relationship with your new IBO.

 Step 4. *Building better teams* both upline and downline, where *T*ogether *E*veryone *A*chieves *M*ore!

As a high *I* style, you will be quick to inspire someone on your team. You may also be quick to *offend* an IBO who has a different style, because your style tends to draw attention to itself as you begin together. If you understand that you will achieve more by focusing on their value to your team, you will have taken an important step as a high *I* style in building a better team. Make it clear that you understand you are not their "royalty", but do give them assignments to read books and listen to tapes, and to write down their questions or ideas. Simply ask them to commit to doing this and then you must commit to discussing it with them. Let them take responsibility for their part in building their business, and be sure to be there to coach whenever they ask.

The high **S** type is a people-oriented, reserved individual. Let's look at how the high **S** type approaches getting started in the business.

Step 1. *Understanding yourself* as the upline, and how your style will naturally approach coaching someone in getting started.

Now that you have been successful in signing a new IBO, as a high **S** type, you will naturally want to be supportive and systematic. The high **S** type is amiable and stable, but will be slow to bring people into their group. You will have reliable answers to provide the new IBO with the information they need to start bringing people into the business themselves. These high **S** type strengths can serve you well. Out of control, however, these same strengths can become areas of struggle that can hinder your success. You will need to understand the importance of reaching out and sharing the opportunity and the system on a regular basis. As a high **S** type, you will naturally want to move routinely through the system, securing the benefits of the different products so you can be loyal to the products, before you share it with another person. Take the initiative to practice stepping just a little outside the limits of your comfort zone, and you will experience a deep sense of fulfillment and satisfaction at what you accomplish. You will find that it will pay off with big success.

Step 2. *Understanding another person* as a new IBO and how their style will naturally approach getting started.

If your new IBO has a high **S** style, they will naturally want to please you. They will need for you to share with them how much you appreciate anything that they do correctly. They will be hesitant and uncomfortable making the changes you are asking of them. In your coaching, you will need to be affirming and kind, giving them time to process the system core materials, and support them with the information, answers, reasons, and business support materials that will empower a high **S** type to get results. Several IBOs have told us that they must be sensitive to encourage questions from a high **S** style, then offer them specific answers. This will empower their systematic style. Be a supportive leader, and they will work hard to produce great results!

Step 3. *Adapting your style to have a better relationship* with your new IBO.

As a high **S** style, you will systematically develop a plan to be successful. You will get started slowly and steadily, and expect your new IBO to do the same. If your new IBO has a different style, you may be really frustrated if they jump right in and demand bottom-line answers; talk a lot, but do little; or want to study the system to death! Since high **S** types naturally appreciate being with people, you will want some of the other styles in your group! Try to be flexible with them, for you will find that their strengths will better build your team and will make you more successful in building a strong business. Work with them according to their styles to help them get started. Coach them by showing the Plan with them and encouraging their efforts. Your example, along with developing an attitude of teamwork, will be the start of a better relationship with your new IBO.

Step 4. *Building better teams* both upline and downline, where *T*ogether *E*veryone *A*chieves *M*ore !

As a high **S** style, you may be hesitant to ask someone to join your team. You may also be hesitant to *offend* an IBO who has a different style, because high **S** types tend to be poor starters as you begin together. If you understand that you will achieve more by accepting other styles on your team, you will have taken an important step as a high **S** style in building a better team. Make it clear that you understand you are not their "servant", and give them assignments to read books and listen to tapes, and to write down their questions or ideas. Simply ask them to commit to doing this, and then you must commit to discussing it with them. Let them take responsibility for their part in building their business, and be sure to be there to coach whenever they ask.

The high **C** type is a task-oriented, reserved individual. Let's look at how the high **C** type approaches getting started in the business.

Step 1. *Understanding yourself* as the upline, and how your style will naturally approach coaching someone in getting started.

Now that you have been successful in sponsoring a new IBO, your high **C** style will naturally want everyone to be conscientious and correctly conform to the system. The high **C** type is cautious and calculating, and will be meticulous as they bring people into their group. You will have comprehensive answers to provide the new IBO with the information they need to start bringing people into the business themselves. These high **C** type strengths can serve you well. Out of control, however, these same strengths can become areas of struggle that can hinder your success. You will need to understand the importance of allowing for the feelings of others while applying the system that your organization is presently using. Your high **C** style will naturally want to be precise and orderly, exploring every possible question, before intensely applying the proven system of your organization. Your high **C** style needs to validate that the system only works with people, and accept that people will usually be less than perfect. You will find that it will pay off with big success.

Step 2. *Understanding another person* as a new IBO and how their style will naturally approach getting started.

If your new IBO has a high **C** style, they will naturally want comprehensive explanations and consistent logic as they learn the system. They will be very teachable initially, but difficult to satisfy if you point out their errors once they have decided that they understand. In your coaching, you will need to be prepared to give them the correct answers that will allow them to discover their own mistakes, and offer them the information, answers, reasons, and business support materials that will empower a high **C** type to get results. Several IBOs have told us that they gather a complete package of materials to validate the specific answers to the questions of the high **C** type. This will empower their conscientious style. Be a consistent leader, and they will work hard to produce great results!

Step 3. *Adapting your style to have a better relationship* with your new IBO.

As a high **C** style, you will carefully develop a plan to be successful. You will get started cautiously and correctly, and expect your new IBO to do the same. However, if your new IBO has a different style, you may be really frustrated if they jump in and ask questions afterwards; talk a lot, but do little; or hesitate to do anything at all! Since high **C** types want long-term business benefits, you will need some of the other styles in your group! Try to be compassionate and allow for their mistakes, for you will find that their strengths in other parts of building your team will make you more successful in building a strong business. Work with them according to their styles to help them get started. Coach them by showing the Plan with them and encouraging their efforts. Your example, along with developing an attitude of teamwork, will be the start of a better relationship with your new IBO.

Step 4. *Building better teams* both upline and downline, where *T*ogether *E*veryone *A*chieves *M*ore !

As a high **C** style, you will be cautious to ask someone to join your team. You may also be critical and *offend* an IBO who has a different style, because your style looks for things to correct as you begin together. If you understand that you will achieve more by welcoming them on your team, you will have taken an important step as a high **C** style in building a better team. Make it clear that you understand you are not their "corrector", but do give them assignments to read books and listen to tapes, and to write down their questions or ideas. Simply ask them to commit to doing this, and then you must commit to discussing it with them. Let them take responsibility for their part in building their business, and be sure to be there to coach whenever they ask.

GETTING PEOPLE ON YOUR TEAM

When you bring a new IBO into your organization, you are asking them to become a part of your team. A true team is formed when two or more people interact freely and personally to accomplish something together. Interacting freely means that team members are comfortable with one another. They feel so secure that they do not protect or filter their contributions. They interact personally, knowing that the other team members will not personally attack them, because they value their unfiltered contributions. Within the framework of this interaction, the team synergy accomplishes something greater than any one team member alone might do!

How does someone become part of your team? It starts as you understand another person better. You will begin to see your differences in a different light. In essence, this means exercising your ability to communicate effectively and act intelligently by adapting your words and actions to their style so that you can meet their needs.

The process of adapting is vital to getting people on your team. Once someone has been sponsored as an IBO, this individual will begin to be part of the team. You now start the process of *Adapting your Style to Have Better Relationships,* to meet their needs and value them as a new member of your team.

STYLES AND DIFFERENCES

No matter how nice they are, sooner or later, a Sponsor and an IBO will begin to see how different they really are. Sometimes they appreciate the variety of their experience, education, or achievements. Other differences can create conflicts. These conflicts usually occur because of differences in personality styles. Different personality styles have different basic priorities, different foundations for their perspectives and choices. The four basic priorities are Power (**D**), People (**I**), Pace (**S**), and Procedure (**C**). These basic priorities will usually surface in one's decision-making style; communication style; or leadership style. Comparing priorities of the high and low types will easily reveal just how different we can be.

Basic Priorities

A **High** *D* prefers to exercise *power* to personally decide because they want to solve problems; they decide for themselves and everyone else.

A **Low** *D* prefers to exercise *power* to personally participate because they want to be a team player; they participate as the group decides.

A **High** *I* prefers to be with *people* to talk because they want to persuade others; they talk things out.

A **Low** *I* prefers to be separated from *people* to listen because they want to be persuaded alone; they think things through.

A **High** *S* prefers a slow *pace* and to keep a routine because they want to maintain predictability; they want a stable, unchanging environment.

A **Low** *S* prefers a flexible *pace* to accommodate change, because they want to be spontaneous; they want variety.

A **High** *C* prefers *procedure* according to facts, because they want to uphold principles; they want data, structure and order.

A **Low** *C* prefers *procedure* according to their feelings, because they want self-expression; they want to be free-spirited.

If one person makes a decision according to facts and principles, while another person makes that same decision according to their feelings and self-expression, is it hard to imagine that they will feel that they are radically different? How could these two people begin to find agreement? They will be more likely to find conflict! We must understand that successfully working through this natural conflict is the first phase that leads to real teamwork and communication. This is difficult work, but the results are rewarding.

No two people are exactly alike; in every relationship, people will have differences. In any beginning relationship, each person values something attractive, but different about the other, so they are willing to **tolerate** other small differences. At some point in the relationship, one or both persons find some difference that is not so small or so attractive. Because of an important difference in their basic priorities, one or both of them are not willing to **tolerate** the other person any longer. When they choose not to **tolerate**, the only other choice is to **eliminate** the difference by **eliminating** the person! These phases in a relationship are shown in this chart:

Phase 1. TOLERATE - Our initial, natural response is to *tolerate* a person's differences. We can put up with, overlook, or ignore those differences, hoping that the other person will get smarter, or learn from our example, or figure things out. We do this for a while, even without understanding *DISC*.

Phase 2. ELIMINATE - Our second natural response is to try make the other person act more like us. In other words, we try to pressure the other person into becoming more like us, which we are sure, would make *them* much happier. Based on our style, we try to pressure them to eliminate their differences in the following ways:

A High **D** demands his/her own way—dominating the other person through the forceful *power* of the **D**s will.

A High **I** emotionally attacks the other person — embarrassing the other person in front of *people*.

A High **S** supports their own *pace*; ignoring, slowly pacifying or placating the person, hoping the problem will go away.

A High **C** avoids a confrontation whenever possible — demonstrating through facts and upholding principles that the **C**s *procedure* is superior.

These phases occur not only in business relationships but also in personal relationships. Think just for a moment of married couples who have fallen in love, gotten married, and are happy to tolerate each other's differences at first. After some period of time, these happy couples started to attack each other, trying to eliminate the differences in the other person. Often this ends in divorce when they simply choose to eliminate the relationship. Business relationships are often more easily eliminated. How can we survive this elimination phase? We can **DISC**over that our unique personality differences are just what make us a great **TEAM**!

Phase 3. APPRECIATE - Understanding the **DISC** Model of Human Behavior, we can raise our **PQ**. This empowers us to see our differences not as right or wrong, good or bad, but simply different! Actually, the other person really *does* see what you see. They simply see it from a different perspective, according to their different priority. Remember the priority for each type: **D** – Power; **I** – People; **S** – Pace; **C** – Procedure. We learn that each type brings a valuable perspective to any given situation. At that point, we can begin to understand how to **appreciate** those differences.

Phase 4. CELEBRATE - As we **appreciate** differences in others, we can learn to value each other and **celebrate** our differences. This is when the real payoff begins! We become a real team when we actually value each team member and enjoy **celebrating** our differences rather than trying to make everyone just the same.

STYLES AND CONFLICT

This next chart deals with the way we tend to respond to conflict. Conflict is caused by the way we choose to address issues because of natural personality differences. When we are unable or unwilling to reach agreement or understand the choices of others, we find ourselves in conflict. Our first response to conflict is **avoidance**. We choose to **avoid** that person and to stay with those who think as we do. When this becomes impractical, our next response to conflict is to **attack**, hurting the other person, sometimes even destroying the relationship. Understanding **DISC** helps us to understand our differences so that we can understand the *cause* of the conflict. This allows us to find common ground and enables us to resolve the conflict. We can then grow in the relationship, **adjusting** ourselves to the differences that created the conflict in the first place. At that point, we can **accept** the person when we truly see the valuable contributions made because of their differences.

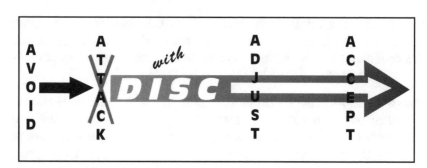

Phase 1. AVOID - Our natural response is to **avoid** the conflict by being around and talking to those individuals who agree with us. Inevitably we must face the conflict.

Phase 2. ATTACK - As we face the conflict, our next response is to **attack** the other person. This will hurt and eventually may destroy the relationship.

> A high **D** will attack the issue with *power, deciding* they must have everything their way and demanding it now! They feel that they have lost the control they need.
>
> A high **I** will emotionally attack the issue, and try to *talk* until they *persuade* the other *person* into their point of view. They feel that they have lost the approval they need.
>
> A high **S** will attack the issue by stubbornly slowing the *pace* and silently *keeping their routine* and doing it their own way. They feel that they have lost the stability they need.
>
> A high **C** will attack the issue by demanding answers, to reconcile conflicting *facts* that disturb them. In this way, they can restore the *procedure* that will *uphold principles*. They feel that they have lost the correctness they need.

When different styles attack like this, the relationship is often hurt and can eventually be destroyed. Understanding **DISC** can preserve the relationship by helping us to understand ourselves and others so that we can raise our **PQ** and move into the next phase, learning to **adjust**.

Phase 3. ADJUST – By understanding the **DISC** Model of Human Behavior, we are able to **adjust** our style. We can learn to better understand ourselves, understand the other person, then adapt our style to meet their needs. This empowers us to improve our relationship instead of destroying it.

Phase 4. **ACCEPT** - This is the phase where we **accept** the resolution to the conflict, and **accept** the other person regardless of the conflict. We begin to value the contributions of the other individual through their unique style. This is when *Together Everyone Achieves More!*

The positive and negative results of recognizing differences and working through conflicts can be clearly seen in this recent example. We were doing some teambuilding for a company. One of their managers had to deal with differences and resolve conflicts with two employees. The employees handled their issues differently, and the results were very different. This study shows a contrast in *PQ* and teambuilding.

A manager, whom we will call Drew, was working with two very different employees. Drew has a *D/S* style blend with a midline *I*. Because Drew has a high *D*, he worked for results, but his secondary high *S* meant he was also very supportive of the employees who reported to him. Eddie reported to Drew. Eddie has a high *I* style with a low *C*. Eddie's high *I* caused him to talk a lot, wanting to be the center of attention and to persuade everyone to his point of view. He preferred a procedure based on his feelings alone. Because he has a low *C*, and didn't like any restrictions, structure, deadlines, or boundaries placed on him. The blend of these types made Eddie expect to express his point of view through total creative freedom in his work.

John also reported to Drew. John has a high *C/D* style blend. John's high *C* style wanted structure and order. Because he also has a high *D*, John would drive hard, to uphold principles and deal with facts for correct procedures. This blend made it difficult for John to work with people. His natural approach to people was critical, judgmental and defensive.

As Drew began to manage Eddie, they first tried to *tolerate* their differences. Eddie talked a lot to Drew and Drew listened. Drew would then directly tell Eddie how to handle the work, because Drew understood that Eddie needed help in staying on task. Although Eddie wanted to do things his own way, to *avoid* a conflict with Drew he mostly did what Drew told him to do. However, Eddie did it only when he felt like he was in the mood to do it.

We introduced **DISC** to their team. When an important project was assigned to their team, and Drew tried to be supportive and give Eddie some creative freedom in how to work on the project. Eddie instead expected to have total creative freedom, and he began to try to *eliminate* this difference with Drew. He told Drew that Drew was wrong and tried to persuade Drew that he must be able to act on his impulses and express himself in the project. Drew listened until he felt that the project was going in the wrong direction. The conflict over the direction that the project would take was important, and the *attack* started.

Eddie *emotionally attacked* Drew, yelling at him and finding every possible way to verbally hurt Drew. Drew responded by *demanding* that Eddie support what he had told him to do. Drew was determined to finish the project, so he decided specifically what Eddie must do to finish it. Eddie walked out and defiantly refused to do anything Drew demanded. Eddie would not adjust, so Drew knew that he would have to finish the project another way. Because Eddie refused to **DISC**over the value of his manager, he *eliminated* their relationship.

John has a very different personality style from Eddie, so naturally Drew had a very different relationship with John. Both Drew and John were predominantly task-oriented, but Drew expected quick results and John expected correct results. They could *tolerate* these differences, except in the part of John's job that involved dealing with their customers. John naturally preferred strict procedures and wanted everyone to follow the rules. He could be critical and cold with customers who came to him feeling that they needed him to do something special for them. Drew just wanted quick results, so he tried to *eliminate* John's procedure if it would better service the customer. This drove John crazy!

They came to us to help them **DISC**over how they could resolve this conflict. We helped Drew and John realize that they both could *appreciate* the fact that the other person really did want to satisfy their customers. Drew **DISC**overed that he often decided that doing something special for a customer would support the customer, keep his loyalty and quickly solve the problem. John **DISC**overed that he thought the customer should understand the company procedure and be satisfied by following it.

Drew and John talked about how their actions had affected each other and the customer. Drew decided that he needed to better manage John in his dealings with people. John asked for a procedure to follow so that he could learn to satisfy the customer's needs. Drew *accepted* that John really struggled with understanding the feelings of the customer. What John needed was a procedure that would help him to address the feelings of the customer.

On the other hand, John accepted that Drew struggled with ignoring procedures in solving problems. Coaching John to value the customer's feelings and coaching Drew to value John's consistency and procedure helped them both to raise their **PQ**. Their relationship was strengthened, and this put Drew and John together on a real team.

In this study, one relationship was *eliminated* because Eddie would not *adjust* and raise his **PQ**. The other relationship grew stronger, because they each raised their **PQ** and *adjusted* to empower their strengths and help the other person where they struggled. Building a team is never easy, but it is worth the work.

PERSONALITY STYLES AND EDUCATION

Teaching styles and learning styles vary because different personality types have different ways of organizing, presenting, processing, and storing information. You will need to work with each person in the way that is most effective for them. Some people will love the educational and motivational tapes. Others may prefer books. Some will learn best at meetings where they have the opportunity to associate with their upline leaders. A few may think education is a waste of time and will have to be shown over time the important benefits they can receive from educational materials.

Each of you has an organization with a highly-tuned system that is a successful. Those who plug in will find the power! One Diamond uses this analogy to explain what the support system does:

An old fisherman survived 14 shipwrecks and was asked if he was a good swimmer. He said, "No. The swimmers think they can make it on their own. They rely on themselves, and they wear out and drown. I just look for something bigger than myself and hang on until somebody comes and rescues me."

For people who are willing and ready to be educated, the support system serves that function. It maximizes the areas of strength while it limits the impact of the struggles. You can learn from the mistakes of others so that you do not have to repeat them! In your own experience, you may have seen that each style tends to take instruction differently:

EDUCATING THE HIGH ***D*** TYPE

High ***D*** styles tend to act decisively, rather than think thoroughly. They respond to whatever works, with their eyes on immediate results.

They want to make their own choices. They did not get into the business to have a boss or a manager. They respond better to challenges than to orders. For example, you can expect better success by *asking* them, "How many of these tapes can you listen to this week?" rather than *telling* them, "You need to listen to these tapes this week."

They plan strategically and can change plans easily if it serves them to do it. They will remember only the most important factors, not all the details. Unless they write it down and tell you that they will contact you with any change of plans, do not expect them naturally and easily to keep commitments. Ask them to repeat back to you for your understanding what you together have decided to do.

Whenever possible, they delegate details. Encourage them at least to understand details for themselves, so they can keep control of situations that may arise. Paperwork is a necessary evil to the high ***D***. They need a straightforward, quick process to complete this task successfully.

Educating the High *I* Type

High *I* styles tend to do what they feel is popular, and to react rather than respond. Because they are impressionable, they like the "new and improved" and tend to take things at face value. It is important for them to look good in front of others.

They prefer to influence people through their charm and humor, rather than by following an established pattern for success. They need to know that you respect them and their abilities. If they feel that you do not take them seriously, they will drift away. They speak glibly when under pressure, trying to use humor to smooth over any difficulty. They are usually very talkative, and they would prefer to keep a friend rather than make a sale. For this reason, they will benefit from receiving instruction on posture, the needed ingredient that will help them keep the friend *and* make the sale! Posture is learning how much to say, as well as what not to say. Encourage the high *I* to be more focused.

Association with leaders is important to them because they like to be able to drop names and tell exciting stories. They tend to be self-promoting, and they need help in demonstrating patience with others who do not bend readily to their influence.

They tend to relate any topic of conversation back to themselves, and others may see them as self-absorbed. They are fun loving and expressive, so they tend to have a wide variety of friends and they make friends easily. They often speak before they have thought through an appropriate response. Listen as they think out loud, and they will tell you what they understand.

EDUCATING THE HIGH **S** TYPE

High **S** styles prefers a slow pace, using the tried and proven for predictable results. They are hesitant starters, but once they start, they can follow through to finish well.

Caring and compassion are important to them, and they often speak up for unrepresented people. They want to consider the feelings of others in any decision. They tend to take excuses a bit too easily and worry about being too pushy with people in their group. They often will do things themselves rather than imposing on someone else to do them.

They prefer to be dedicated followers and do not seek out leadership roles. However, they can make good leaders because they like to include everyone. They will not ask anyone else to do what they would not do themselves. They place high value on appreciation and gratitude.

Do not expect them to speak up if they are offended, because they are not comfortable in confrontations. Give them time to adjust to changes. They have a difficult time saying *no* to any requests. Encourage them to become more assertive and less tentative, and support their correct decisions.

EDUCATING THE HIGH **C** TYPE

High **C** styles tend to be rational responders, rather than emotional reactors. They love to uphold principles, and they respond well to a logical, fact-based approach.

Often, they put correctness ahead of other values, and they evaluate character and reliability by the consistency of each person's actions. Because they discount feelings in any situation, it is easy for them to come across as critical and cynical.

They tend to dwell on details and want to see the whole picture before moving ahead. They take paperwork very seriously and like things to be well organized. They like rational, objective presentations of data and do not want to be caught in an error.

They tend to see things in black and white terms of "either/or" and "true/false." They prefer a slower pace that allows them to categorize information, and they become skeptical when rushed through this process.

Security is vital to them, and they tend to cut off people whom they see as frivolous, insincere, or threatening. They dismiss whatever they see as fanciful or exaggerated.

They do not respond well to emotional appeals, which they view as manipulation. Encourage them to begin to recognize their feelings and the feelings of others in order to relate to other people more effectively.

NEVER TOO LATE

If you have been an IBO for awhile and think it is too late for "Getting Started with Style," we are pleased to tell you that it is never too late! Just as you can pick up this book and start understanding yourself, you can pick up your dream and start working to achieve it. This time around, your higher *PQ* is an added advantage!

If you are coaching someone who feels like a football player who has missed the first half and is coming into the game late, this little story may help them to be encouraged:

The annual football game began between the Big Animals and the Little Animals. The Big Animals always expected to win because they always had such a physical advantage. During the first half, they ran up and down the field at will. Then, the second half began. This time, they were unable to advance the ball. No matter which Big Animal got the ball, it tripped and fell, right at the line of scrimmage. Finally, the Big Animals looked down and saw a little centipede, wearing a tiny helmet with the team colors of the Little Animals. The quarterback for the Big Animals asked, "Are you making all those tackles? How come we never ran into you in the first half?" And the little centipede replied, "I was tying my shoes!"

 **TAKE ACTION**

You can and will make a difference once you get in the game, too!

If you feel like you have been in the game all along, but you feel you have not yet scored, keep playing. Remember these words from a nineteenth century writer, Elbert Hubbard:

> *The line between failure and success is so fine that we scarcely know when we pass it; so fine that we are often on the line and do not know it.*

We must learn to say with Zig Ziglar:

> *I am not going to give up, back up, let up, ease up or shut up until I am taken up!*

CHAPTER FOURTEEN

PERSONAL ACTION PLAN

Question 1: If you have recently sponsored a new IBO, list three important points from this chapter that you can remember to raise your **PQ** and communicate with that person more effectively as they get started in the business. _____

_____

_____

_____

Question 2: If you are still waiting to sponsor a new IBO, list three important points about your personality style that will help you get a better start in the business._____

_____

_____

_____

Question 3: From the *Styles and Differences* section in this chapter, describe, in your own words, your Basic Priority and how this issue is most important to you._____

_____

_____

Building a Team with Style

What makes a great team? Is it the star player? Is it the coach? Is it the game they play? A great team has all of these great elements, but there is something about a group of players working together that creates something better than any one of them alone could create. We call that something *teamwork*. A great coach creates an atmosphere within the team where each player knows their importance to the team. Each player is motivated to give their best! Have you ever had a great coach? Dr. Rohm remembers:

> I had a great coach in high school. His name was Chris Jones. He became the most influential person in my life. Coach Jones came to me one day and said, "Did you hear about Raymond Berry?" My heart sank. At that time, Raymond Berry was a great End for the Baltimore Colts football team. I was sure that some tragedy had occurred, and I really looked up to Raymond Berry. In shock, I said, "No! What happened?" Coach Jones replied, "He just retired today!" I guess I was glad that he had not been in some big accident, but still my heart sank. Raymond Berry was one of my heroes, and he was quitting the game. To my surprise, a grin began to spread across Coach Jones' face. He declared, "I bet they draft you right out of high school to take his place!"
>
> I still wear a smile when I think of what that did for me. What a great coach! He gave me the recognition I needed. He thought I could replace Raymond Berry! He believed in me, so I played my heart out for him on that football field. When I did, I gave more to my team than I ever dreamed that I could!

One of the great geniuses of the business you are building is that it is structured to make teamwork happen. Your upline can be *your* coach, and *you* can be the coach for your downline.

The benefits of coaching from your upline include:

- Getting experienced advice for making attainable plans
- Receiving a different perspective on your actions or words
- Having someone who cares about you and your business
- Knowing someone to help you avoid pitfalls, but who will help you recover if you stumble into one
- Developing a long-term relationship for fun and effective interaction and growth

As you meet your upline Direct and others in your upline who are successful in the business, cultivate a positive relationship with them. Dr. David Schwartz says in his book, *The Magic of Thinking Big*, that we should actively seek advice from successful people.

> *Make it a rule to seek advice from people who know. There's a lot of incorrect thinking that successful people are inaccessible. The plain truth is that they are not. As a rule, it's the more successful people who are the most humble and ready to help. Since they are sincerely interested in their work and success, they are eager to see that the work lives on, and that somebody capable succeeds them when they retire. It's the "would-be-big" people who are most often the most abrupt and hard to get to know.*

In our business, your upline coaches are not only *interested* in your success, but they *have an interest* in your success. When they give you good coaching and you follow it successfully, your success gives them financial reward, too.

RECEIVING COACHING FROM YOUR UPLINE

When you receive coaching, raise your *Personality Quotient* to see how your personality style reacts and interacts with your upline's personality style. For greatest effectiveness, understand your personality struggles and learn to get them under your control. Understand the Basic Priority of your upline, and appreciate your differences. You can draw from their strengths as they coach you! Start with *PQ* Step 1 *Understanding yourself through your personality style*:

If you have a high D style: Receiving coaching is sometimes hard for a high *D*, since they naturally make decisions to make things happen. They naturally come to their own decisions quickly, so they will have to make a conscious decision to listen to their coach. Once the *D* has decided to be coached, they will begin to appreciate the benefits they receive. It may be a hard step to take, but it will be worth the effort.

PQ Step 2 *Understanding another person through their personality style* shows how the coaching **you receive** will be affected by your upline's style as well. Looking back over this book to get a picture of their style will help you to understand their perspective. Now you can begin *PQ* Step 3 *Adapting your style to have better relationships.* Here are some tips for adapting your style when you receive upline coaching

D **Coached by a *D***: Tell your upline what you would like to discuss. You will see "eye-to-eye" pretty quickly. Give your upline your attention, and they will share valuable information with you. Since you have similar personality styles, you can learn from their mistakes, and duplicate their successes.

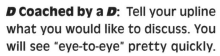

D **Coached by an *I***: Be friendly with your upline to set them at ease. Let them teach you by telling stories and giving examples. Remember that people are their priority. Expect them to be a little less businesslike, and understand that the best information you glean from them may come over lunch or at an unexpected moment. They can show you how to attract people to your business.

D **Coached by an *S***: Consciously control your energy level to slow down a little bit! Let them know that you appreciate them and ask them gently for their insights. They will need time to warm up to your latest idea. Give them time to digest any information by suggesting that they can think about a situation and respond to you at your next meeting. Remember that pace is their priority, and respect their steadiness. They can show you how to keep people in your business.

D* Coached by a *C: Expect them to ask for specific, detailed information. Make the effort to think critically with them about your business. Respect the energy that they expend as they think through principles that they may understand and value more fully than you do. Ask them questions about procedures. They will predict pitfalls that you are not aware of in building your business.

Page 242 gives us a ready reference for the high *D* receiving coaching from the others styles.

When you receive coaching, raise your *PQ* to see how your personality style reacts and interacts with your upline's personality style. For greatest effectiveness, understand your personality struggles and learn to get them under your control. Understand the priority of your upline, and appreciate your differences. You can draw from their strengths as they coach you! Start with *PQ* Step 1 *Understanding yourself through your personality style:*

If you have a high *I* style: You will love a good coach! Your coach can help you focus your excitement to improve your performance. You will naturally have fun with your coach, so you will need to focus on taking time to listen and really understand the coaching they are trying to give you. Give them a chance to talk, then tell them what you understand about what they said. Coaching can be a fun experience for you as you learn and apply new ideas.

PQ Step 2 *Understanding another person through their personality style* shows how the coaching you receive will be affected by your upline's style as well. Looking back over this book to get a picture of their style will help you to understand their perspective. Now you can begin *PQ* Step 3 *Adapting your style to have better relationships.* Here are some tips for adapting your style when you receive upline coaching...

I* Coached by a *D: Ask them to lunch. Remember that power is their priority. Appreciate that their businesslike approach will help you become more focused. Ask them direct questions, and then take responsibility to do something with the answers they give you. Expect a high **D** leader to challenge you— show them what you can do! Work with them, so that you can ask them to have some fun with you in the business, too!

I **Coached by an *I*:** This will be fun, for sure! You just need to help each other remember to talk about business. This coach will tell stories that you will remember and from which you can learn. Since you have similar personality styles, you can learn from their mistakes, and duplicate their successes. Make an effort to recognize something you want from your meeting. Write down what you have learned. Talk to someone about it and do something with it! How exciting to build the business with them!

I **Coached by an *S*:** When you reach out to them, they will receive you warmly, but you will earn their trust by respecting their priority for a slower pace. Enjoy talking with them, and give them time to talk to you! Then give them time to respond to you. Remember that they will not be pushy, but they will be slow to accept change, regardless of your enthusiasm. Appreciate the stability that they can give you as you build your business.

I **Coached by a *C*:** Consciously control your excitement, and be a little more serious! Prepare for your meeting by writing down a few specific questions to give to them. Give them space, physically and verbally, so that they can develop a proper relationship with you. Try not to fidget or play with objects out of nervous energy; this may upset their concentration. Ask them for an example if you are unsure of what they mean when they answer your question. Repeat to them what you feel they expect you to do, so that you have the same understanding. Make an effort to follow through responsibly. Appreciate the credibility that they can give you as you build your business.

Page 243 gives us a ready reference for the high *I* receiving coaching from the other styles.

When you receive coaching, raise your **PQ** to see how your personality style reacts and interacts with your upline's personality style. For greatest effectiveness, understand your personality struggles and learn to get them under your control. Understand the priority of your upline, and appreciate your differences. You can draw from their strengths as they coach you! Start with **PQ** Step 1 *Understanding yourself through your personality style*:

If you have a high S style: A Coach can help you get started by appreciating your skills, ideas, and attitudes. Your coach will affirm the importance of following the system. They will help you try new products and talk to new people by doing it with you! They will be a friend who cares about you when you are hesitant, and will help you to learn to be more confident. Together, you will become part of a great team!

PQ Step 2 *Understanding another person through their personality style* shows how the coaching you receive will be affected by your upline's style as well. Looking back over this book to get a picture of their style will help you to understand their perspective. Now you can begin **PQ** Step 3 *Adapting your style to have better relationships*. Here are some tips for adapting your style when you receive upline coaching.

S Coached by a D: Listen carefully to their direction, and ask them to repeat anything you do not understand. Tell them that you would like time to process the information they are giving you and request that you may revisit the topic at your next meeting. Remember that they want you to be successful, so be confident in talking with them. Because their priority is power, they may challenge what you do or say. They are not trying to intimidate you, they simply want to know what you really believe and are committed to do. Appreciate the drive that they can give to you as you build your business.

S Coached by an I: Because you both like people, you should naturally be able to relate well. Enjoy listening to your coach's stories, and build your confidence by hearing how the system works. Ask their permission to revisit a topic that you would like some time to think about. They will easily give that permission, but realize that you will need to bring the subject up again because they will probably forget. Appreciate the enthusiasm that they can give to you as you build your business.

S Coached by an S: This will be such a caring team! You will both need reassurance and will appreciate each other. Let them show you how they got started, and ask them to help you build confidence. You will naturally be good friends. They can help you learn to deal with other personality styles more easily. Since you have similar personality styles, you can learn from their mistakes, and duplicate their successes.

S Coached by a C: You will appreciate their more reserved approach to the business. Remember that their priority is procedure, so allow them to set the agenda for your meetings. Ask them to plan, as part of their agenda, for you to have some time to process information. They will ask questions, and may seem skeptical of your answers. This is a result of their intensity as they deal with facts, not because they do not like you. When you come to agreement about something, repeat to them your understanding of what you are to do. Ask them to clarify any possible misunderstanding. Appreciate the accuracy they can give you as you build the business.

Page 244 gives us a ready reference for the high **S** receiving coaching from the others styles.

When you receive coaching, raise your **PQ** to see how your personality style reacts and interacts with your upline's personality style. For greatest effectiveness, understand your personality struggles and learn to get them under your control. Understand the priority of your upline, and appreciate your differences. You can draw from their strengths as they coach you! Start with **PQ** Step 1 *Understanding yourself through your personality style:*

If you are a *C*: A Coach will enjoy working with you since you tend to be very well organized. You will want to understand and correctly follow the procedure for building the business. You will easily master the paperwork and procedures. Your coach can help you begin to understand how to appreciate the feelings of others as another factor in building the business. You probably tend to believe only what you can understand and validate, so you are more comfortable working with facts and data. Your coach will help you understand how to do things properly within the system and to learn how to be flexible with people for long-term success in the business!

PQ Step 2 *Understanding another person through their personality style* shows how the coaching you receive will be affected by your upline's style as well. Looking back over this book to get a picture of their style will help you to understand their perspective. Now you can begin ***PQ*** Step 3 *Adapting your style to have better relationships.* Here are some tips for adapting your style when you receive upline coaching...

C* Coached by a *D: This coach is task-oriented, like you are, so you will get right down to business! They will head right to the bottom line, so ask them for support materials to provide the details you need to understand. Understand that their priority is power. They may make a wrong decision because they decide quickly, but they have no qualms about changing the decision to get the results they want. This procedure will be difficult for you to accept. Ask them for time before your next meeting to validate the course of action they suggest, by reading the support material or talking with someone who can give you more details. This time delay will be difficult for them to accept. Appreciate the results they can bring to building your business.

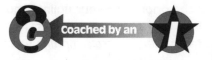

C* Coached by an *I: Relax a little, and smile to let them know that you care about them. As they talk, learn to listen through their emotion for the facts you want and the procedure you need. You will best communicate a question or idea to them by trying to explain your concept in story form or by relating it to their experience. Remember that their priority is people, so develop a procedure for relating to them that is positive and energetic. Talk about something you are learning from support materials, or someone you met at a function. Let down your guard and enjoy yourself. Appreciate the fun they can bring to building your business.

C **Coached by an** *S*: Return the friendly warmth that they offer you to let them know that you care about them. Ask about their family, and talk about yours. Remember that their priority is pace, so be sensitive to take the time they need in your procedure. Ask for their help in specific ways; they will want to help, and you will want specifics. Appreciate the warmth they can bring to building your business.

C **Coached by a** *C*: This coach will find answers to all your questions! Because you both make procedure your priority, you will logically take one step at a time and plan for long-term success. Ask for their experienced help in building relationships with people who do not share your style. Since you have similar personality styles, you can learn from their mistakes, and duplicate their successes.

The chart on page 245 gives us a ready reference for the high *C* receiving coaching from the others styles.

REMEMBER **D**s...
DECIDE TO RECEIVE
YOUR COACH!

Learn from their example
Give them your attention
Avoid confrontation

Learn to relax
Give friendly eye contact
Avoid missing their story lessons

Learn to use their details
Give room for procedures
Avoid the pitfalls they see

Learn to slow down
Give reassurance
Avoid driving over them

REMEMBER *I*S...
OPENLY RECEIVE
YOUR COACH!

Learn to focus with them
Give them a lunch invitation
Avoid too much storytelling

Learn from their successes
Give them a chance to talk
Avoid pointless chatting

Learn to control your excitement
Give them space
Avoid fidgeting

Learn to respect their pace
Give them time to talk
Avoid emotional appeals to them

REMEMBER **S**s...
CONFIDENTLY RECEIVE
YOUR COACH!

Learn to listen for direction
Give feedback for understanding
Avoid tuning them out

Learn about the system through stories
Give a timed response
Avoid being simply entertained

Learn to ask for time to respond
Give them information
Avoid uncertainty from their coolness

Learn from their successes
Give reassurance
Avoid slowing each other down

REMEMBER **C**s...
KINDLY RECEIVE
YOUR COACH!

Learn to ask for business
support materials

Give summary statements

Avoid irritation by recognizing
results

Learn to hear facts through
their emotions

Give them a smile!

Avoid underestimating them

Learn to ask for their specific help

Give friendly warmth

Avoid getting lost in the details

Learn from their successes

Give real life questions

Avoid perfectionism

COACHING DOWNLINE

These tips for coaching someone in your downline are not intended to tell you what to say. They are, instead, suggestions for how to adapt your style so that you will communicate effectively with them. These four charts will provide a ready reference for your approach to each **DISC** type. Keep in mind that most people have personality styles that are a blend of at least two high types, so also consider their secondary high types as you approach working with them. For instance, you would relate to someone who has an **I/D** style blend in a manner that is different from an **I/S** style blend.

For in-depth information on the style blend differences, see *Who Do You Think You Are, Anyway...?* (pp.256 - 324) by Dr. Robert A. Rohm, available from Personality Insights, Inc.

When you are coaching, raise your **PQ** to see how your personality style reacts and interacts with your downline's personality style. For greatest effectiveness, understand your personality struggles and learn to get them under your control. Understand the priority of your downline, and appreciate your differences. You can empower their strengths through your coaching! Start with **PQ** Step 1 *Understanding yourself through your personality style*:

If you have a high D style: You are confident and decisive, and may be bored by details. As a result, you may quickly change a plan of action to get the results you wanted. Your priority is power. You like new and innovative things and respond to challenges. Handling several issues at once energizes you, so your body language can be intimidating. You can be aggressive and demanding, and will be naturally dominant in any setting.

PQ Step 2 *Understanding another person through their personality style* shows how the coaching you give will be received by your downline's style. Looking back over this book to get a picture of their style will help you to understand their perspective. Now you can begin **PQ** Step 3 *Adapting your style to have better relationships.* Here are some tips for adapting your style when you are coaching downline...

D Coaching a D: You can be direct with another high **D**! They will be decisive, so provide options and choices for them. Offer any information from your experience, and ask them to tell you if they decide to change their decision. Coach them in understanding their personality style by sharing with them your strengths and struggles. Talk with them about how others may perceive your driving style.

D Coaching an I: Be friendly and let them know that you enjoy their fun-loving style! Go to lunch with them and they will enjoy the interaction. Appreciating their priority for people means that they want you to like them, so listen to their stories and direct their attention to something they can learn from what they have shared. Suggest tapes or other support materials from people they know, or that you would like them to know. You may feel that they are unfocused, but do not talk down to them. Direct their enthusiasm toward action, and ask them to tell you what they did! Talk with them about your personality style, and let them know that you want to help them get results in the business.

D Coaching an S: Make a conscious decision to slow down, to be more friendly and less forceful. Listen to them carefully and do not interrupt them. Give them the time they need to digest the information you are providing. Ask them to offer their input at your next meeting. Remember their priority for pace means that they will not be pushed, and they like to know that something is proven and predictable. Too much change will make them simply shut down, so be patient with them. Show genuine appreciation for their people-oriented style. Talk with them about your personality style, and let them know that you want to help them get results in the business.

D Coaching a C: You are both task-oriented, so expect intense interaction with them! Provide them with as many support materials as are available to you so that they can validate your information. They will want to talk to you about more data and facts than you think they need for any decision, but listen to them to understand their progress on their decision. Let them know that you appreciate their need to be correct, and encourage them to improve with practice. If they have made a mistake, tactfully suggest an area they might "recheck," rather than pointing out where they were wrong. They will probably want a proper distance between you, so respect their reserved nature and hold back a bit. Talk with them about your personality style, and let them know that you want to help them get results in the business.

Page 255 gives us a ready reference for the high *D* coaching downline.

When you are coaching, raise your *PQ* to see how your personality style reacts and interacts with your downline's personality style. For greatest effectiveness, understand your personality struggles and learn to get them under your control. Understand the priority of your downline, and appreciate your differences. You can empower their strengths through your coaching! Start with *PQ* Step 1 *Understanding yourself through your personality style*:

If you have a high *I* style: You love being with people! You like to have fun and talk a lot. You are naturally inspiring and interesting, so the talking part of coaching will be easy for you. Learning to listen in order to satisfy the needs of your downline will be more difficult for you. Your mood may swing from elation to boredom easily, so you will need special effort to follow through on something you enjoyed talking about. This effort will make your coaching more effective, as you are inspiring in any setting.

PQ Step 2 *Understanding another person through their personality style* shows how the coaching you give will be affected by your downline's style. Looking back over this book to get a picture of their style will help you to understand their perspective. Now you can begin *PQ* Step 3 *Adapting your style to have better relationships.* Here are some tips for adapting your style when you are coaching downline...

I **Coaching a *D*:** Talk about how to get results with people. Because their priority is power, they will want you to give them choices. They value solid options over soft opinions. Limit your stories to the topic under discussion. Ask them to lunch, and set apart your time in advance. In your conversation, if you feel their frustration rising, ask an open probe instead of talking. Then listen and think. Let them know that you believe in them. Close the conversation confidently with a written plan of cooperation, action, and responsibilities. Talk with them about your personality style, and let them know that you want to help them bring people into the business.

I **Coaching an *I*:** This will be fun, for sure! Let them know in advance what you want to accomplish. Keep an eye on your time and priorities for the meeting. Recognize their achievements and accomplishment, the encouraging aspects of their learning experiences. Show them how you use short-term goals and small, immediate rewards to make your work fun. Offer tapes with exciting stories from people whom you would like them to know. Let them know that you believe in them. Coach them in understanding their personality style by sharing with them your strengths and struggles. Talk with them about how others may perceive your fun-loving style.

I **Coaching an *S*:** Your people-oriented styles will naturally interact well. Respect their priority for pace and slow down a bit to set them at ease. Enjoy talking with them, and be sure to give them time to talk. Let them know that you appreciate them and want to help them. Give them information, and time to process that information before they must respond. Ask them if they would be comfortable with making plans at your next meeting, then make a note to do it. Look for small agreements, not big changes. Talk with them about your personality style, and let them know that you want to help them bring people into the business. Follow up the meeting with an Amvox message that is affirming and friendly.

I **Coaching a** *C*: A *C* may seem to enjoy your natural style of establishing a relationship by telling stories and making things fun. To gain credibility with them, however, you will need to learn to respect their priority for procedure. Simply put, they will not trust you unless you focus on follow through. Offer them support materials with facts and data instead of giving them a generalization to answer a question they ask. Be careful to do what you say you will do, for you may forget, but they will remember. A handshake is a proper greeting for them; let them make any move to offer personal information, too. Let them know that you appreciate their accuracy and critical-thinking skills. Ask what they think about any story you tell, and be prepared to listen. Explain that you tend to think out loud, but understand that they tend to arrive at a conclusion before they say anything. If they *have* made a mistake, tactfully suggest an area they might "recheck," rather than pointing out where they were wrong. Close your meeting with a list of things you have accomplished or have agreed to do, with a copy for each of you. Talk with them about your personality style, and let them know that you want to help them bring people into the business.

Page 256 gives us a ready reference for the high *I* coaching downline.

When you are coaching, raise your *PQ* to see how your personality style reacts and interacts with your downline's personality style. For greatest effectiveness, understand your personality struggles and learn to get them under your control. Understand the priority of your downline, and appreciate your differences. You can empower their strengths through your coaching! Start with *PQ* Step 1 *Understanding yourself through your personality style:*

If you have a high *S* style: Your style can naturally be an effective salesperson because you are so customer-focused. People tend to trust you because you are steady and dependable, but you may miss an opportunity to close if you hesitate to ask. You naturally invest yourself in others, but people may impose upon you too easily. Let them take responsibility for their actions. "Nature abhors a vacuum," so if you do not lead confidently, others will gladly take the opportunity. You are sympathetic and can come alongside someone for effective coaching. If you can learn to project confidence when asking for a commitment, people will more readily say *yes* to you, because you are supportive in any setting.

PQ Step 2 *Understanding another person through their personality style* shows how the coaching you give will be affected by your downline's style. Looking back over this book to get a picture of their style will help you to understand their perspective. Now you can begin **PQ** Step 3 Adapting your style to have better relationships. Here are some tips for adapting your style when you are coaching downline...

S Coaching a D: Because of their naturally decisive style, you can say to them just what is on your mind. They want you to *quit circling and land*! You will hesitate to confront them for any reason, while they seem to make anything into a confrontation. Remember that their priority is power, so they simply want to solve the problem by deciding what to do. Give them acceptable options, and do not avoid leading them. Choose your words to project confidence, so they will listen and give you the respect they want to give you. Ask them directly for time to process information they give you. Get their commitment to talk to you if they decide to change plans that you have made. They are like high-flying kites, and you are the string that keeps them safely anchored, able to fly without crashing. Talk with them about your personality style, and let them know that you want to help them bring security into the business.

S Coaching an I: You both have people-oriented styles, so you will probably enjoy each other. As the coach, you will want to listen to the *I* talk, noting areas of concern they may mention. Draw their attention to examples or stories that can help them. They talk a lot, and you will tend to remember more than they will, so help them follow through after their good intentions have worn off. Suggest business tapes of heart-warming stories that you would like them to hear. Appreciate their enthusiasm and expressive communication. Help them focus on a course of action to take after your meeting. Talk with them about your personality style, and let them know that you want to help them bring security into the business.

S Coaching an S: You will make each other comfortable and become fine friends. Small courtesies mean a lot to them, as they do to you. Let them know that real leaders in the business are servants, helping others succeed. Tell them how you moved beyond your misgivings to do things you found difficult in establishing your business. Encourage them to try what worked for you. They love to hear, "We are doing fine." Coach them in understanding their personality style by sharing with them your strengths and struggles. Talk with them about how others may perceive your reserved and supportive style.

S Coaching a C: Your reserved manner will work well with this IBO. Because of their priority for correct procedure, they will not be convinced by "the way it has always been done." They will need support materials to validate your information, and you will gain credibility with them if you give them permission to validate information before planning further. They will respond well to your encouragement, and will think about what you say. Talk with them about your personality style, and let them know that you want to help them bring security into the business.

Page 257 gives us a ready reference for the high **S** coaching downline.

When you are coaching, raise your **PQ** to see how your personality style reacts and interacts with your downline's personality style. For greatest effectiveness, understand your personality struggles and learn to get them under your control. Understand the priority of your downline, and appreciate your differences. You can empower their strengths through your coaching! Start with **PQ** Step 1 *Understanding yourself through your personality style*:

If you have a high C style: You enjoy planning and procedure, and need to be organized. You look for order in life and may discount feelings because they do not easily fit into this paradigm. You study facts and figures to validate information, but your intense focus may cause you to miss the larger perspective. Your standards are high, so you have great confidence in your products, but you may need to show more confidence in your people. As a coach, others will depend on your credibility, because you will be conscientious in any setting.

PQ Step 2 *Understanding another person through their personality style* shows how the coaching you give will be received by your downline's style. Looking back over this book to get a picture of their style will help you to understand their perspective. Now you can begin **PQ** Step 3 *Adapting your style to have better relationships*. Here are some tips for adapting your style when you are coaching downline...

 **C Coaching a D**: You are both task-oriented individuals, so your interaction will be intense! Remember their priority is power, so they will naturally be decisive in order to solve problems. Provide correct choices for them, but do not let them put you to work for them. Offer information as soon as they ask for it, but keep the bottom line in mind and be as brief as possible. Understand their view of goals: They tend to write their goals in concrete and their plans to get there in sand, while you set your goals in sand and set firm plans in concrete. Talk with them about your personality style, and let them know that you want to help them bring conscientiousness into their business.

 **C Coaching an I**: Their instinctive speech patterns may overwhelm you, for they seem to talk about everything! Try to listen for a line of reasoning, and draw attention to the point of their story by asking an open probe question. Explain a concept to them by using a story they may relate to. Put anything you expect them to do in writing, with a copy for both of you. Admit that you are less than perfect, and allow them to be less than perfect, too.

Suggest tapes or other support materials from people you may know, or that you would like them to know. Talk with them about your personality style, and let them know that you want to help them bring conscientiousness into their business.

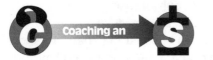

C **Coaching an** *S*: Your reserved manner will relate well with this IBO. Begin your conversation warmly by inquiring about family or mutual friends. Listen for signs of struggles, and try to be encouraging with your words. You will naturally make a plan for your meeting, but be flexible to meet their needs. Share the truth with them in a tactful manner. They will appreciate your kindness more than your correctness. Ask them if they need help with anything, and encourage them to trust the system so they can be more comfortable as they build the business. Talk with them about your personality style, and let them know that you want to help them bring conscientiousness into their business.

C **Coaching a** *C*: You will both be satisfied with the correct procedure! Your only challenge may be that you will both try to find the in-depth meaning of the in-depth meaning. Plan your meetings so that you can remember to keep the larger perspective in mind. It may be difficult to admit that you are less than perfect, but by doing this you can help them accept that they are less than perfect, too. Being able to relax can make you both more accessible to people. Encourage them by telling them how you practice showing the Plan. Coach them in understanding their personality style by sharing with them your strengths and struggles. Talk with them about how others may perceive your cautious style.

Page 258 gives us a ready reference for the high *C* coaching downline.

REMEMBER **D**S...
DECIDE TO COACH
ACCORDING TO
THEIR STYLE!

Lead with options
Listen for their decisions
Respect their drive for results

D coaching a D

Lead with a friendly
focus
Listen to their stories
Respect their enthusiasm

D coaching an I

D coaching an S

Lead with slowed,
friendly pace
Listen without
interrupting
Respect their steadiness

D coaching a C

Lead with business support materials
Listen for their logic
Respect their consistency

REMEMBER *I*S...
MAKE YOUR FUN
ACTUALLY WORK!

Lead with solid options
Listen after your open probe
Respect their vision

I coaching a D

Lead based on your success
Listen so they can talk
Respect their interest in people

I coaching an I

I coaching an S

Lead with friendly conversation
Listen to their responses
Respect their slower pace

I coaching a C

Lead with credible follow through
Listen for their expectations
Respect their procedures

REMEMBER Ss...
SUPPORT THE SYSTEM
AND THEIR STYLE!

S Coaching a D

Lead showing your purpose
Listen for their decisions
Respect their problem-solving ability

S Coaching an I

Lead with focus toward actions
Listen to their stories for feelings
Respect their intentions

S Coaching an S

Lead by your example
Listen and affirm them
Respect their thoughtfulness

S Coaching a C

Lead them with validation
Listen and encourage them
Respect their conscientiousness

REMEMBER Cs...
WARM UP TO
COACHING THEM!

C coaching a D

Lead with correct options

Listen to their plans and offer suggestions

Respect their hard work

C Coaching an I

Lead with story concepts

Listen for a line of reasoning

Respect your written agreement

C Coaching an S

Lead with encouragement

Listen for signs of struggles

Respect their calmness

C coaching a C

Lead by your example

Listen for the larger perspective

Respect their carefulness

As you receive coaching and coach others, you will practice raising your **PQ** and learn how to communicate effectively with many different people. You will understand yourself and the unique strengths you can offer to your business team. You will celebrate the different gifts your spouse also contributes to the team. You will understand from experience the value that each personality type brings to the business. You will experience the teamwork that makes the dreamwork!

As we begin the twenty-first century, technology has *dissolved* the distance barrier to communication. We can use e-mail to send an instantaneous message almost anywhere in the world. We can now explore more information on the Internet than most people in the past had available to them over their entire lives. At the same time, technology has sometimes *increased* the distance barrier to effective communication. There is something about seeing a person's face, hearing their response, and talking to them in person that simply cannot be simulated with our modern technology. Remember the last time that you got a recording on a telephone response system? No matter how hard they tried to communicate with you, talking to a machine is just not the same as talking to a person, *in person*!

As our business goes increasingly electronic, we must also become more skilled at maintaining effective communication and developing our people skills. The chart on the following page is meant to give you a picture of how the general population will approach Quixtar. If you will notice, 35% of the population is task-oriented by design, while 65% of the population is people-oriented. This is very important to understand. The task-oriented individuals will naturally gravitate toward exploring and using the new technology, while the other 65% will want to see people, not talk to a computer. These people-oriented individuals will need extra education, motivation, and understanding to bring their friendly orientation into our electronic business. Our team needs these people more than ever! Keep this picture in mind and review these helpful tips as we enter the twenty-first century.

STRENGTHS OF THE TASK-ORIENTED STYLES

Want Better Choices/Changes for Products
Lead/Explore What's New
Protect Products
Are High Tech
Are Technical
Are Focused
Value Logic
Need Information

35% of IBOs see *TASK* first

D — 10% of Population

C — 25% of Population

Deliver the Goods!
Talk about great results!
Show how easy ordering means
speedy delivery of quality goods!
Make sure the new system really works.

WAYS TO OVERCOME THE STRUGGLES OF THE TASK-ORIENTED STYLES

Strengths of the People-Oriented Styles

**Want Better Look/Feel for Products
Excitement/Enjoy What's New
Protect the People
Are High Touch
Are Relational
Are Enthusiastic
Value Feeling
Need Application**

30% of Population

35% of Population

**65% of IBOs
see
PEOPLE first**

**Deliver the fun!
Talk about great experiences!
Show how easy ordering
means sharing with more people!
Make sure to keep in touch with them.**

Ways to Overcome the Struggles of the People-Oriented Styles

A TAKE ACTION

CHAPTER FIFTEEN

PERSONAL ACTION PLAN

Question 1: Discuss three tips you can use to more effectively receive coaching from your upline.

1. _____

_____

2. _____

_____

3. _____

_____

Question 2: Discuss three tips you can use to more effectively coach downline.

1. _____

_____

2. _____

_____

3. _____

_____

Question 3: Using Chart page 261-262, discuss your strengths and struggles as you start using Quixtar with your upline.

Successful Business Building Styles

Dr. Rohm was speaking at a weekend Diamond function recently. He had introduced **DISC** personality types, and we were enjoying talking with many IBOs at our book table. As Stewart was talking with one IBO, he asked a question we had heard before as he said, "You can be honest with me, and it won't hurt my feelings if you tell me the truth... Can somebody with *my* style actually build the business?"

Stewart was happy to assure this IBO that any personality style can build the business! He thanked Stewart for the hope he offered, and said that he could not wait to hear the final session with Dr. Rohm. As you have learned so much more about **DISC** personality types in this book, we want to make sure to offer this hope and reassurance to you and anyone you coach.

Building your business depends on raising your **PQ** to understand yourself, to understand the IBOs in your organization, to adapt your style to have better relationships with them, and to build a great business team! Every personality style has strengths to offer their team; every personality style also has struggles, but can find another team member's strength that will help them. No one can build the business alone. We need each other to be successful. Remember that all of us are better than one of us!

THE **TEAM** QUESTIONS

If you want to become part of a great team, ask yourself these questions:

"Am I reading the books my upline Diamond is recommending?"

"Am I listening to tapes on a consistent basis?"

"Am I learning to show the Plan and adding to my list of names?"

"Am I attending every function I am qualified to attend?"

"Am I taking my questions to my coaching upline to receive encouragement and instruction?"

When you can answer "Yes!" to all these questions, you can be sure that you are following the correct procedure to build the business. You will be empowered to establish security and get results as you bring people into the business! You will become a vital part of your team!

Surprising Statistics

In corporate America, the vast majority of Fortune 500 companies are headed by high *D* leaders. Incidentally, an unusually large number of them were in the Marine Corps! Because of this, we expected to find a very large percentage of Diamonds and Emeralds that would also reflect this high *D* style. To this date, over 1,000 IBO leaders have completed our Profile Assessments, and we wondered what this would tell us about their styles. How did the styles of these leaders compare with the styles of the general population? Did a majority of these IBO leaders have a high *D* style like the leaders of the Fortune 500 companies?

Here is what we found:

All the *DISC* types had fairly equal representation among the Diamonds and Emeralds! You do not need to have a high *D* style, or any other specific style to have a better advantage in becoming an IBO leader.

In the general population, about 35% have a task-oriented style. Among corporate leaders, the *vast majority* has a task-oriented style. But among IBO leaders, about *half* had a task-oriented style.

In the general population, about 65% have a people-oriented style. *Very few* corporate leaders would have a people-oriented style. But among IBO leaders, about *half* had a people-oriented style.

In the general population, about 40% have an outgoing style. Among corporate leaders, a *vast majority* has an outgoing style. But among IBO leaders, about *half* had an outgoing style.

In the general population, about 60% have a reserved style. *Very few* corporate leaders have a reserved style. But among IBO leaders, about *half* had a reserved style.

We understand that, in corporate America, being a successful leader usually means having a high **D** style. In our business, however, we **DISC**overed that people with every personality style had built the business to levels of significant success! What style can build the business? Yours can!

For more detailed information on these statistics, reference the seventy page appendix in *Who Do You Think You Are, Anyway?* by Dr. Robert A. Rohm, available from Personality Insights, Inc.

SUCCESSFUL PEOPLE SELECT THEMSELVES

As we have had the privilege of meeting and working with many Diamonds, we have realized that these highly successful Independent Business Owners have picked themselves to succeed from every possible personality style. No one else picked them.

- Some high **S** and **C** styles chose to step out and lead when they might have felt more comfortable remaining in the background.

- Some high **D** and **I** styles chose to step back and serve when they might have felt more comfortable at the forefront.

- Some high **D** and **C** styles chose to involve themselves with others when they might have felt more comfortable by concentrating on tasks.

- Some high **I** and **S** styles chose to focus their activity toward goals and results when they might have felt more comfortable interacting socially.

Remember that every personality type has its own strengths and struggles. Even if you had a different style, you would just have a different type of strengths and struggles with which to deal. W. Clement Stone, the billionaire insurance executive and founder of *Success* magazine, tells us:

All personal achievement starts in the mind of the individual. Your personal achievement starts in your mind. The first step is to know exactly what your problem, goal or desire is. If you're not clear about this, then write it down, and rewrite it until the words express precisely what you are after.

No one has accomplished measurable success in any area of life without developing additional skills, or without acquiring traits that seem to be more natural to other people with different personality styles. Hang on to your dream and start to grow!

A CATEGORY ERROR

When you think about it, how could any *one* style have the majority of attributes that make for Diamond-level success? If someone asks, "What personality style should I be to build my business?" he or she is making a category error. It's like asking, "What does the color blue taste like?" It's a question without a real answer...

The question on which your success hinges is: "I understand my personality style. What can I be doing with it to build my business?" As you understand the style of your upline, you can learn to adapt to have a good relationship with them. They will coach you to duplicate their pattern, not imitate their style. As we heard one leader tell his organization, "*You* need to be *yourself* more than you need to be your Diamond!"

PLAY TO YOUR STRENGTHS

A professional baseball pitcher was acquired by a team because of his impossible-to-hit fast ball. But he spent all of his warm-up time working on his weak curve ball. No matter how much he practiced, it was not as strong as his fast ball. Finally, the team's manager forced him to concentrate on his strengths. He said, "I didn't trade you for your curve ball, hoping it would get better. I traded you for your fast ball, what you do best!"

What a great coach! Your biggest successes will come as you raise your **PQ**, check your signals, balance your style, use your strengths, depend on your team and give it your best! It's not what you have, but why and how you use it that counts! President Harry Truman wrote:

> *I studied the lives of great men and famous women, and I found that the men and women who got on top were those who did the jobs they had in hand, with everything they had of energy and enthusiasm and hard work.*

BECOMING YOUR BEST

Learning to understand yourself and others is so much fun! Knowing how to adapt your style in order to work well with others can shorten your path to success at any level. Recognizing the strengths others bring to your team will begin to help them build the business with you, too. Because we have seen Diamonds do it—with strengths and struggles that are much like your own — we know that you can do it, too!

As Dr. Rohm says at the close of his program

Sponsor with Style:

Remember this:

It's not which style you have,
but how you use it that counts.
I can learn to adjust who I am...
to become all I need to be!

CHAPTER SIXTEEN

PERSONAL ACTION PLAN

In the Introduction, Dr. Rohm challenged you to make a commitment to use one new concept from your Personal Action Plan each week. In this way, you will practice over 50 success strategies for buliding you business in this year!

Pick one concept from the book that was especially meaningful to you, and then discuss it here. Also write down how you can practice this concept this week. Have a great time as you Sponsor with Style!

_____

_____

_____

_____

_____

_____

_____

_____

Understanding Your Graphs

If you have completed an Adult Profile Assessment or a Computer Profile Assessment like the Successment, or Managing for Success, take a few minutes to find the two graphs in your assessment and transfer them to this page. This will give you a reference in your book as we talk about your personality style.

If you have not completed a personality profile assessment, please call us at 1.800.509.DISC and we will be happy to take your order over the phone. If you prefer, you may also use the order form in the back of this book.

GRAPH I – ENVIRONMENT ("MOST" TOTALS HERE)

PERSONALITY STYLE	D	I	S	C
HIGH	20, 16, 15, 14, 13	17, 10, 9, 8, 7	19, 12, 11, 10	15, 9, 8, 7
FAIRLY HIGH	12, 11, 10	6, 5	9, 8	6
AVERAGE (Slightly Above)	9, 8, 7	4	7, 6, 5	5
MID-LINE	6, 5, 4	3, 2	4, 3	4
AVERAGE (Slightly Below)	3, 2		2	3, 2
FAIRLY LOW	1	1	1	1
LOW	0	0	0	0

GRAPH II – BASIC STYLE ("LEAST" TOTALS HERE)

PERSONALITY STYLE	D	I	S	C
HIGH	0, 1	0, 1	0, 1, 2	0, 1, 2
FAIRLY HIGH	2, 3	2, 3	3, 4	3
AVERAGE (Slightly Above)	4, 5	4	5, 6	4, 5, 6
MID-LINE	6	5		7
AVERAGE (Slightly Below)	7, 8	6	7, 8	8
FAIRLY LOW	9, 10, 11, 12	7, 8	9, 10	9, 10
LOW	13, 14, 15, 16, 21	9, 10, 11, 19	11, 12, 13, 19	11, 12, 13, 16

Now that you have transferred your graphs, we will spend a few minutes to learn what they might tell you about your personality style! One graph is your response to **Environment, Graph I**, and the other is your **Basic Style, Graph II**. Let us introduce you to each of these.

GRAPH I is your **Response to Environment** graph. This graph shows *the way you have learned to function in your environment in order to achieve success.* Your environment influences why you choose to act the way you do. Psychologists often refer to this as "nurture." Your environment often changes, due to your life stage, your changing role requirements, or major life-changing events. Therefore this graph tends to be more changeable over time. We all seek to adapt or adjust our behavior throughout life as situations or circumstances require. For example, do you need to be very decisive in your current environment? In your Response to Environment graph, this would tend to make your **D** type higher.

You will notice that **GRAPH I** has the word "MOST" printed above it. This graph is derived from the phrases you selected in the "MOST" category in the Style Analysis. A simple illustration will explain why the Environment graph comes from your MOST choices. What do you MOST want for dinner tonight? You may feel like having pizza; you may want a steak dinner; or you may really want a seafood salad. Your "MOST" choice is influenced by your current environment: pizza by take-out would be quick, and you are really busy tonight. Finishing a special project, or celebrating a birthday may change your choice to a steak dinner. On the other hand, you may be in the mood for just a seafood salad. When you know what your environment calls for or demands, you are better equipped to make more appropriate choices. Your most choices are more affected by your environment, which is usually more changeable. Also notice that the plotting point numbers on **GRAPH I** are shown from **high** at the top to **low** at the bottom. The more choices you made for each **DISC** type, the higher your plotting point for that type.

GRAPH II is your **Basic Style** graph. This graph shows how you are "wired", exhibiting your natural behavior. This is how you tend to behave when you are totally at ease. It is the behavior you will gravitate to when you are under pressure because it is where you feel safest. It is how you naturally respond to something or someone. To a certain degree, your personality is formed by your genetic makeup. Your unique DNA chain contains genetic characteristics from many generations, which are part of your personality make up. You are designed a certain way from birth, before any outside influences occur. Psychologists often refer to this as "nature." This graph will remain more constant throughout life.

You will see that **GRAPH II** has the word "LEAST" printed above it. This graph reflects your selections from the "LEAST" category — what you said you are *least* like. Remember our dinner illustration? What if you were given the dinner choices of pizza, a steak dinner, or seafood salad, but you *hate* seafood? Chances are good that you would choose seafood as your least desireable choice. You probably would not change that choice, no matter where you were. You are usually very consistent in the things you do not like. This is the correlation with your LEAST choices. The fewer times you chose a *D*, *I*, *S*, or *C* as your "LEAST" response, the higher that type is plotted on **GRAPH II**. These plotting point numbers are charted from **fewer** at the top, to **more** at the bottom. For **GRAPH II**, look at your plotting point **locations** (high or low) rather than your plotting point **numbers**, in order to compare your two graphs. Both graphs will probably be fairly similar in appearance.

Understanding **DISC** Types and Your Personality Style

Your graphs are based on the **DISC** Model of Human Behavior. This model shows that human behavior can be described as either Outgoing or Reserved. It can also be described as Task-oriented or People-oriented. When placed on bisecting quadrant lines, we see the four types like this:

Dominant **D** - Your need for personal **Power**
Inspiring **I** - Your need to interact with **People**
Supportive **S** - Your need for a predictable **Pace**
Cautious **C** - Your need for strict **Procedure**

If your **D** is high, the **D** plotting point on your graph is in the upper segment of the graph.This means you are **Dominant** in your personality style. If your **D** is low, that means you are low in dominance, and tend to let others take the lead. If your **D** is close to the midline, you are average in that type, sometimes choosing to be dominant, while at other times not. Your plotting point position shows the intensity of the **D** type in your personality style. The higher that plotting point is, the stronger that type is in your personality style. These intensity levels will also be true for your **I**, **S**, and **C** plotting points as well.

You may also compare the locations of the plotting points on the two graphs. If the location of the **D** plotting point on your Response to Environment (Graph I) is similar to the location of the **D** plotting point on your Basic Style (Graph II), we may conclude that you feel that your natural style works well in your current environment. The **DISC** scores in these two graphs simply indicate the difference in how you *choose to respond* in your environment, versus how you *naturally respond*. The more these two graphs are alike, the more harmony you feel with the behavior your environment requires. The more these two graphs differ, the more you are making an effort to adapt to your environment and the more uncomfortable you probably feel. Most people will have similar graphs, although often there are one or two plotting points that are in significantly different segments. If, for example, your **C** is much higher in your Basic Style (Graph II) than in your Response to Environment Style (Graph I), you feel that your current environment requires you to be less cautious than you might naturally be.

These guidelines will help you interpret your *Style Analysis* graphs. For a more indepth discussion of **DISC**, or to understand your graphs more completely, the books ***Positive Personality Profiles*** and ***Who Do You Think You Are, Anyway***? can be obtained from Personality Insights, Inc.

Personality Insights Order Form

Your name – please print   Company name

Your mailing address – street or post office box

Your city, state, zip code

Credit card number   Expiration date   Name on card

Quantity	Description	Unit Price	Total
BOOKS			
_____	Sponsor with Style	14.95	_____
_____	Positive Personality Profiles	11.95	_____
_____	Who Do You Think You Are, Anyway...?	14.95	_____

PERSONALITY PROFILE ASSESSMENT

_____	New Interactive Adult Profile Assessment	10.00	_____
_____	Successment ™ Computer Report	30.00	_____

SUPPORT MATERIALS FOR SPONSOR WITH STYLE

_____	Power Plan Pages for your Planner	10.00	_____
_____	Sponsor with Style Video Seminar	20.00	_____
_____	Sponsor with Style Funbook	3.00	_____
_____	Sponsor with Style Leader's Kit	259.00	_____

With 3 SwS Funbooks - Retail Vaule $9.00
And 1 SwS video (used with Funbooks) - Retail Vaule $19.95
And 3 SwS books - Retail Vaule $44.85
And 3 Power Plan Pages - Retail Vaule $30.00
And 3 PV cubes - Retail Vaule $30.00
And 3 Successments (computerized profiles) - Retail Vaule $90.00
With leader's Guide - Retail Vaule $59.95

LEARN HOW TO TEACH THIS TO YOUR GROUP

_____	Sponsor with Style Training Conference	495.00	_____

(two day interactive conference includes Leader's Kit)

TOTAL ORDER .... $_____

ADD 10% FOR SHIPPING AND HANDLING (**$3.00 minimum**) .... $_____
(Canadian shipping and handling $4.00 minimum)

TOTAL BY CHECK OR CREDIT CARD .... $_____
(Georgia Residents also must add applicable sales tax on Total Order amount)

PERSONALITY INSIGHTS

P.O. Box 28592 • Atlanta, GA 30358 • 800-509-3472 • Fax 770-509-1484

website at www.personality-insights.com

PLEASE REQUEST OUR LATEST CATALOG OF ADDITIONAL PRODUCTS
FOR FAMILY & BUSINESS THAT WILL EMPOWER YOU TO IMPROVE